THE LANGUAGE OF COMMODITIES

A Commodity Glossary

Rosemary Erickson

George Steinbeck

New York Institute of Finance

Library of Congress Cataloging in Publication Data

Steinbeck, George.
  The language of commodities.

  1. Commodity exchanges—Dictionaries. I. Erickson,
Rosemary. II. Title.
HG6046.S67 1985   332.64′4′0321   85-7213
  ISBN 0-13-521717-2

© 1985 by New York Institute of Finance

This publication is designed to provide accurate and authoritative information in regard to the subject matter covered. It is sold with the understanding that the publisher is not engaged in rendering legal, accounting, or other professional service. If legal advice or other expert assistance is required, the services of a competent professional person should be sought.

—*From a Declaration of Principles jointly adopted by a Committee of the American Bar Association and a Committee of Publishers and Associations*

Printed in the United States of America

10 9 8 7 6 5 4 3 2 1

New York Institute of Finance
(NYIF Corp.)
70 Pine St.
New York, New York 10270

Preface

The once small market place where agricultural products were traded is no more. The commodity industry has grown into many large, complex, and unique markets with

- seemingly endless product introductions,
- new and changing regulations, and
- new participants continually entering into this wonderful, exciting world of commodities.

Each contributes to the growth of something else: *the language of commodities*.

No doubt about it, even the most seasoned individual will be faced with new and arcane terms.

How does one keep up?

This work is meant to aid you in doing just that. The need is evident.

Key words and phrases were selected from the futures, options, forwards, and actuals markets. Commonly used terms of peripheral industries—such as shipping, import and export, insurance, banking, and credit—were included as they relate to our industry.

These terms were then carefully researched and discussed to determine the meanings as they relate to our industry. Although every effort has been made to assure valid, authoritative definitions, be aware that they may represent the authors' interpretation and should not be considered a "legal" definition. The authors are not lawyers but individuals who daily live in the world of commodities.

This glossary is intended for use by anyone who needs—or simply wants—a clear, easy-to-understand source of terms used in the industry. Therefore, it will benefit a wide variety of readers—direct participants, those in the peripheral businesses, potential investors, students, teachers, or the person who just likes to know.

Our Special Thanks
We would like to acknowledge the help of several respected individuals of the commodity industry who contributed their personal time and encouragement during the development of this project:

Houston Cox, Angelo LaSpina, and John Mattesich for reviewing the manuscript and providing us with comments and suggestions.

Special mention goes to Charles E. Robinson, Senior Vice President of the Futures Industry Association, Inc. who this time—as always—found the time to contribute invaluable assistance. He is a true benefactor of the commodity futures industry.

How to Use This Book Effectively

Terms

The words, abbreviations, and phrases in this glossary are printed in **bold face** and located at the left margin.

Definitions

One or more definitions in the column to the right of each term.

No judgment has been made.as to the most frequently used definition as the reader would determine which is most commonly used in a particular area. For example, the most frequently used meaning for Actual Price in the futures area would be different from the most frequently used meaning of the same term for a reader in the cash market.

Alphabetization

All terms at the left-hand margin are arranged alphabetically, letter by letter rather than word by word or by main words.

Sometimes several terms in the industry have the same meaning. In such cases, the first term alphabetically carries the definition. All other terms carry a cross-reference to the first term.

Any synonymous term(s) further in alphabetic arrangement are cross-referenced directing the reader to the term carrying the definition.

Cross-References

Cross-references are represented by the word **See** and the term(s) in *italic print*.

This notation following a definition directs the reader to another entry:

- to get additional information on the given term,
- to distinguish shades of meaning between terminology or
- to express an antonym.

This notation following the word alone directs the reader to the synonym carrying the definition.

When more than one term is listed and separated by slashes, the first term carries the definition. When more than one term is listed but with no separating slashes, each term carries a definition.

Example

Examples have been included for further clarification, as necessary.

Appendixes

At the end of this book (page 192) you will find an appendix entitled "How to Read the Commodity Financial Quotes." This is a step-by-step description for reading and using the financial pages of the daily newspaper or screens from retrieval services.

Another appendix, entitled "Basic Calculations" (page 194), demonstrates the use of formulas and calculations done on a daily basis.

The appendix "How to Find a Commodity Factor (page 196) explains how to translate information given in the financial pages into the component used in commodity formulas—"factor."

The appendix called "Reference Guides" (page 197) displays frequently used commodity abbreviations for exchanges, organizations, and ticket symbols.

AA

The standard abbreviation for *Against Actuals*. The exchange of a futures position for the physical commodity made between a buyer and seller.

Also known as: *Exchange of Cash for Futures, Exchange of Spot (for Futures), Exchange for Physicals, EFP, Exchange Against Actuals, Cash Commodity for Futures*

> **Example:** A processor has inventory in storage for needs in the next few months. The processor is approached by another party for supplies and is offered an attractive price. To take advantage of the price and retain the protection of having sufficient supplies when needed, the processor requires a coffee futures contract in return for the physical coffee. The swap is registered with the exchange but is not entered via the trading ring.

Abandonment

The means of giving up the rights of an option by allowing the option contract to terminate on a specified calendar date (the expiration date).

> **Example:**
>
> | Option | Strike | Expiration Date |
> |---|---|---|
> | Long 1 MCH 8X Gold Call | @ 360 | 2/10/8X |
>
> If on 2/10 the price of the futures is below 360, the holder of the option will not exercise his/her right to that futures because to do so would mean to take a built-in loss. By taking no action, the option is allowed to expire as of that date.

For actuals, abandonment is the refusal of a consignee to accept delivery of a shipment that is damaged and considered worthless.

The rights and obligations to the futures or actuals cease to exist.

Also known as: *Expiration*

Acceptance

Agreement of intention to carry out a transaction.

The taking of delivery.

A time draft or bill of exchange on the face of which a drawee writes the word "accepted" along with the date and place of payment.

Accommodation Trade

A prearranged, wash transaction through which one party enters into an order to assist another party to complete an illegal trade.

Account

A customer who buys and/or sells in a commodity market.

Also known as: *Trading Account*

A record of buy and/or sell transactions.

Account Classification

The separation of accounts into categories for easy recognition, especially during internal processing.

> **Examples:**
> Hedger, speculator
> Exchange member

Account Executive

An agent of a commission house who is responsible for dealing directly with the clients for compensation, generally a percentage. Responsibilities could include obtaining required documents, explaining rules and regulations, entering client orders, and giving general information, prices, and market conditions.

Also known as: *AE (the standard abbreviation), Registered Representative (RR), Registered Commodity Representative (RCR), Associated or Approved Person (AP)*

Account Type

An identification commonly used in the operational area to distinguish regulated from nonregulated accounting within the same account number.

> **Example:** A customer trades domestic and foreign commodities. The transactions for the two cannot, by regulation, be placed in the same account. Therefore, two designation identifiers are created and added to a base account number separating the domestic accounting from that of the foreign, while still maintaining one base control number.
>
> ---
> 3875 (acct base) 01 (domestic identifier)
> 3875 (acct base) 02 (foreign identifier)
> ---

Accumulate

A method of adding to a position over a period of time at the same or differing prices during market fluctuations, rather than in one purchase, at one time, at one price.

Active Market

A market of heavy trading.

A market with a large open interest.

Active Trading Months

The months designated by a given exchange for which trading in a given commodity product may be initiated.

> **Example:** Chicago wheat is traded for delivery in the following contract months: March, May, July, September, and December. Trading for March Wheat in a given year can be initiated and/or actively traded

during any calendar month from October (18 months prior to March of the given year) through March of that year.

Months with activity or commitments.

Example: COMEX Gold is permitted to trade in all 12 calendar months. Because of economic or market considerations, the market may not have all 12 months active.

Active	Permitted
January	January
February	February
	March
April	April
	May

March and May do not have an open interest or trading activity. Therefore, although trading is permitted in these months, they are not yet active months.

See: Contract Months/Delivery Months

Actual Price

The price of the actual commodity.

The price at which a futures contract is executed.

Example: Bought at 371 (price).

In a price-setting transaction, the price of one leg of a spread. The price is set at one of the prices traded during the given transaction day.

Example:

Buy 5M May Wheat
Sell 5M July Wheat
10-point spread, May price to be fixed

May traded at 340, 345, 346, 355
July traded at 345, 346

The trader may select any price between 340 and 355 recorded for May as the May actual price and receive the July sale at 10 points over May. The July price must be within the *permitted* July trading range for that day.

See: Price Setting
Possible Price

Actual(s)

The physical or cash (including financial instruments) commodity that is available immediately or within a given period of time.

The basis of a futures contract.

Also known as: Cash Commodity, Physical Commodity, Spot Commodity

See: Futures

ADP

The standard abbreviation for *Alternative Delivery Procedure.* A term of the contract under which the buyer and seller, via their respective brokers on the exchange floor, agree to delivery terms (port, grade, premium, or discount) other than those specified in the contract. Notification must be made to the clearing house.

Example: A traded contract such as crude oil that calls for delivery at a number of facilities in the state of Louisiana may, upon mutual agreement between the buyer and the seller, be changed for delivery in Texas, Oklahoma or New York. All liabilities and responsibilities remain with the two parties.

AE

See: *Account Executive*

Affiliated Person

A party who has ownership or control over a given entity.

An individual associated with a futures commission merchant in a capacity such as partner, officer, director, etc., as defined by the Commodity Futures Trading Commission (CFTC), who thereby falls under the trading regulations and standards of the CFTC but is not required to register with the CFTC as such.

See: *Associated Person*

Afloat

A physical commodity which is in transit on a vessel or in a harbor about to sail but not at the destination.

Against Actuals

See: *AA*

Aging (of Margin Calls)

A method of computing the number of days an outstanding margin call moves from a receivable to a liability status in compliance with the Commodity Futures Trading Commission's regulations.

Example:

Day	Action	Status
Monday	Call issued	Receivable
Tuesday	Call mailed	Receivable
Wednesday	1st day count	Receivable
Thursday	2nd day count	Receivable
Friday	3rd day count	Receivable
Monday	(next business)	Liability

Note: Monday and Tuesday occur on the same business day because the results of Monday's activity are not seen until Tuesday morning.

The example reflects the handling of most common accounts serviced by brokers. Exceptions are explained in the Commodity Futures Trading Commission regulations.

Alternate Delivery Procedure

See: *ADP*

AP

The standard abbreviation for *Associated Person or Approved Person*. An individual who works for a futures commission merchant, commodity trading advisor, and commodity pool operators as an account executive, soliciting and accepting customer orders. An associated person must be registered with the Commodity Futures Trading Commission and is subject to all qualifications and regulations set forth in the Commodity Exchange Act.

(Approved) Delivery Facility

A depository, vessel, equipment, etc., that meets exchange specifications and is deemed appropriate for delivery of the given commodity.

(Approved) Delivery Mechanism

The specified process for delivery of a given commodity, including certificates, documents, and facilities as set by the authorized exchange.

Approved Person

See: *AP*

| **Arbitrage** | A trading technique, utilized by either the speculator or the hedger, that involves the simultaneous purchase of actuals or futures in a given market against the sale of similar or identical actuals or futures in a different market with the expectation that the difference in price between the two transactions will result in a profit. |

Example: A trader believes the price of cash wheat is out of line with the futures market. He/she believes the price levels will narrow (be closer to each other).

| *Cash market* | Buy 5M Wheat | @ 3.75/bu |
| *Futures* | Sell 5M Dec Wheat | @ 3.85/bu |

If the reasoning is correct, and on 12/01 the original position is offset by

| *Cash market* | Sell 5M Wheat | @ 3.80/bu |
| *Futures* | Buy 5M Dec Wheat | @ 3.83/bu |

this trade would yield .05/bu in the cash market and .02/bu in the futures market.

If the reasoning is incorrect and the basis for wheat remains the same through December, the net difference would be zero, with no gain or loss.

If the reasoning is incorrect and the basis for wheat widens rather than narrows against the trade, the net result would be a loss.

See: *Spread(ing)*

Arbitrageur

A trader who uses arbitrage strategy.

See: *Arbitrage*

Arbitration

A system in which a third party negotiates the settlement of a dispute between two other parties. Arbitration is a quasi-legal process but legally binding on the parties involved.

Arbitrator

The individual or panel empowered to settle a dispute in arbitration.

See: *Claimant*
Respondent

Arrival Notice

An import document sent by a carrier informing the party to be notified of arrival date, shipment details, and free-time expiration.

Ascending Triangle

A chart price pattern formed by high prices in the same proximity in advances and low prices moving rapidly higher so that the slope side of the triangle goes in an upward direction. See Illustration A-1.

See: *Descending Triangle*
Pennant/Symmetrical Triangle

Ask(ed)

An indication of willingness, made at a given moment on the floor of an exchange, to sell a specific quantity of a commodity at a specific price.

The price made in the offer.

Also known as: *Offer*

See: *Bid*

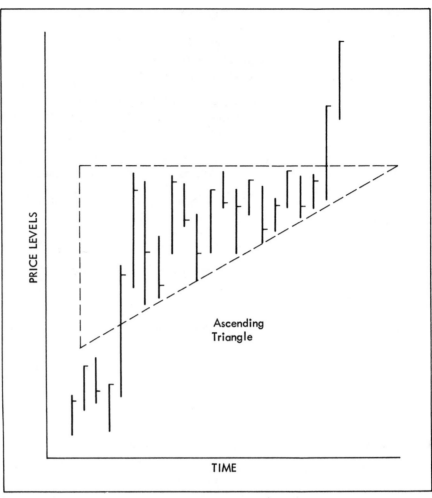

Ascending
Triangle

PRICE LEVELS

TIME

Illustration A-1

As-of Trade

A trade being recorded or booked on a calendar date after the actual execution date.

> **Example:** Trade executed:
>
> 2/17 Bgt 1 Mar Copper 6100
>
> Trade booked and confirmed on the next day:
>
> 2/18 Long 1 Mar Copper 6100 as of 2/17

Assignee

The recipient of the transferred legal rights specified in a (assignment) contract.

See: *Assignor*

Assignment

The conversion of a short option contract to the underlying futures contract at the specified, contracted strike price. A call is assigned into a short futures, a put into a long futures. An assignment is an obligation on the holder of a short position.

> **Example:**
>
> | Option | Strike |
> |---|---|
> | Short 1 Feb COMEX Gold Call | @ 400.00 |
> | Short 1 Feb COMEX Gold Put | @ 380.00 |

upon assignment becomes

Futures	Trade Price
Short 1 Feb COMEX Gold	@ 400.00
Long 1 Feb COMEX Gold	@ 380.00

This term is also used in transferring the rights of an option to the actual commodity.

See: *Exercise*

Assignor

The party that transfers ownership or legal rights in a (assignment) contract.

See: *Assignee*

Associated Person

See: *AP*

Assurance

A legal agreement whereby one party agrees to compensate another party for losses or damages.

The business of providing this protection.

Also known as: *Insurance   The term assurance is more commonly used when referring to marine cases.*

The legal certificate or document which defines and guarantees this protection.

Also known as: *Insurance Policy*

Assured

The party of an insurance contract with the insurable interest or the one who would be injured by loss or damage. (The assured benefits from safe arrival of goods.)

Also known as: *Insured*

See: *Insurer/Underwriter*

At-or-Better

An order carrying a specific price. Execution will occur only at the specified price or a higher one (in the case of a sell, a lower one in the case of a buy).

Also known as: *Or Better Order (OB)*

Example:

Buy 5M May Wheat 330 or better

may also be written as

B 5M K WHT 330 OB

An execution of 330 or any price less than 330 is mandatory if this order is to be executed.

See: *Stop Loss Order*

At-the-Close

An instruction to buy or sell at the best price available during the closing period of the market on a given day.

Also known as: *Market on Close*

Example:

Sell 5M May Wheat Market on Close

may also be written as

S 5M K WHT MOC

The above order can be executed only during the exchange-specified closing period. If the market trades in the range of 350 to 360 during that time, any price in that range can be a trade price. It need not be the very last price traded, nor is it necessarily guaranteed to be the best price of the range.

See: *At-the-Open(ing)*

At-the-Market

An order to buy or sell a specified number of contracts for a specified commodity month at the best price available at the time the order reaches the trading ring.

Also known as: *Market order*

Example:

Buy 5M May Wheat Market

may also be written as

B 5M K WHT MKT

As long as the execution price represents the best offering at the time of execution and the price received was traded approximately at the time the order entered the trading ring, any price is acceptable.

See: *Contingency Order*

At-the-Money

The relationship of an option to the underlying futures contract. Whether call or put, long or short, the strike price of the option is equal to the current price of the underlying futures.

Example:

COMEX February Gold

Futures Settlement for January 4 @ 400.00

Option Strike Price	Call Trade Price	Put Trade Price
380	10.00	2.00
400	1.30	13.30
420	.20	32.20

All calls and puts trading at the 400.00 strike price on January 4 are considered at-the-money. Should the option be immediately exercised, no profit or loss would be realized.

See: *In-the-Money*
Out-of-the-Money

At-the-Open(ing)

An instruction to buy or sell at the best price available during the opening period of the market on a given day.

Example:

Sell 5M May Corn Market on the opening

may also be written as

S 5M K Crn Mkt opening only

Execution can take place only during the exchange-specified opening period. If the market trades in the range of 330 to 335 during that time, any price in that range can be the trade price. Trade price need not be the first price traded nor necessarily be guaranteed to be the best price in that range.

See: *At-the-Close*

At-Sight	A term signifying that payment is due immediately upon presentation of a given document or bill.

Auction (Market)

A system of trading on an exchange floor where buyers and sellers compete via open outcry with other buyers and sellers for the best price. Commodity futures exchanges practice the auction market theory via pit trading.

> **Example:** This method requires two or more participants. Person A bids 100. Person B offers 102. Person C can bid 101, offer 101, sell at 100, or buy at 102.
>
> Persons A and B created the market publicly via open outcry. Person C was given the opportunity to narrow the bid and offer or buy or sell the existing quotes.

See: *Blackboard Trading/Board Trading*

Audit Trail

A means of supporting entries in which references may be traced from each point to the original source.

Authorization to Transfer

A document giving a broker authorization to remove by transfer segregated funds from a segregated customer account to meet debit obligations in non-segregated accounts of that client. This action is limited to accounts for the same customer and can occur only when a debt is due. The document must be signed and dated by the customer.

Note: Margin calls outstanding are considered debt obligations.

Average(ing)

An arithmetic mean obtained by adding two or more items and dividing the sum by the number of items.

Example:

Trade Price
600.00
630.00
690.00

$$\text{Average trade price} = \frac{600.00 + 630.00 + 690.00}{3}$$

$$\text{Average trade price} = 640.00$$

In shipping, a loss of ships or cargo or damage to cargo.

Payments made by owners or insurers.

Buying the same commodity at the same or varying prices over price fluctuations.

See: *Averaging Down*
Averaging Up

Averaging Down

Purchasing or selling additional positions as prices decline.

Example:

Jan 20 Long 1 Apr COMEX Gold 394
Jan 22 Long 1 Apr COMEX Gold 393
Jan 24 Long 1 Apr COMEX Gold 390

Averaging can take place over days, as above; over months; or within minutes.

See: *Averaging Up*

Averaging Up

Purchasing or selling additional positions as prices advance.

> **Example:** A trader believes a recent bull trend is about to reverse. The trader picks a point and sells at 390. The market continues strong. A second sale is made at 490, then at 540. Assuming each trade is one contract, the trader's average price of 473.33 is higher than the initial trade. This activity can be executed over minutes, days, or weeks.

Acquiring additional positions (longs or shorts) using paper profits.

Also known as: *Pyramiding*

> **Example:** An individual buys 5,000 bushels of wheat with a contract value of $27,000 and deposits margin of $2,500 for that contract. If the market goes in favor of the client by 10% ($27,000 × .10), $2,700 in paper profits makes it theoretically possible to purchase an additional contract.

See: *Averaging Down*

Back Spread

A spread, used by arbitrageurs, with a smaller than normal difference in price in two or more currency or commodity markets.

Example:

Normal Price for a Commodity		
U.S.		$ 90.00
London £ 50.00	U.S. $ equivalent	100.00

Current Price for the Commodity		
U.S.		$90.00
London £ 45.00	U.S. $ equivalent	90.00

A trader would Buy London and simultaneously Sell U.S. Assuming the U.S. commodity stays unchanged (at the normal level) and London rises to its normal level, the trader would then Sell London and Buy U.S. No money would be gained or lost on the U.S. trade:

Bought $90.00/Sold $90.00

The London trade would have a gain of £ 5.00 (U.S. equivalent $10.00), resulting in a profit of $10.00.

Bought £ 45/Sold £ 50

Back Month

A calendar month that is active and more than 90 days from the current trading month.

Example:

Active Months	Mar	May	Jun	Jul	Dec
Current Month	Mar				
Back Months				Jul	Dec

Sometimes this term is used to signify a month in which futures trading is taking place with a maturity other than current, spot.

Example:

Active Months	Mar	May	Jun	Jul	Dec
Current Month	Mar				
Back Months		May	Jun	Jul	Dec

See: *Spot Month*

Backwardation

A market in which supplies are currently in shortage, causing the near contract months to sell at premium and distant contract months to sell at discount.

Also known as: *Inverted Market*

Example:

Soybeans	Sep	Nov	Jan	Mar
	5.60	5.49	5.40	5.38

Supply and demand outweigh carrying charges (storage and handling) of the normal market.

A basic pricing structure in which the near deliveries cost more than the futures.

The practice of delaying settlement in the London Market. For backwardation, charges are paid by the seller.

See: *Contango/Normal market*

Balance

To compute the net value of an account.

The net debit or credit money remaining in an account.

See Illustration B-1.

To arrange so that one set of elements equals another.

GENERAL LEDGER ACCOUNT

Control Account	Debit	Credit	Reconciliation
Balance Total Customers		$20,000	$20,000 cr
			$20,000 cr

SUBORDINATE LEDGER CUSTOMER ACCOUNTS

Customer A	Debit	Credit	
Balance		$10,000	$10,000 cr
Customer B	Debit	Credit	
Balance	$5,000		5,000 dr
Customer C	Debit	Credit	
Balance		$15,000	15,000 cr
			$20,000 cr

Illustration B-1

The equalization of ledger monies to unrealized profit and loss of open position inventory.

Balance of Payments   A country's surplus or deficit after all total international transactions. Balance of payments consists of imports and exports of goods, services, and investment capital, as well as international movements of financial reserves.

Balance of Trade   An import or export balance of a country's merchandise transactions. More exports than imports is considered a favorable balance of trade; more imports than exports is an unfavorable balance.

Bank Draft   A sight or demand order drawn on a bank (drawer) by another bank (drawee).

Banker's Acceptance   A negotiable time draft or bill of exchange resulting from either domestic shipping or any import or export transactions in which a bank accepts the obligation to pay the seller if the buyer defaults.

Bar Chart   A graph of horizontal bars or vertical columns comparing characteristics of two or more items or showing differing proportions of those items. Bar charts are used in technical analysis to track price ranges and movements. See Illustration B-2.

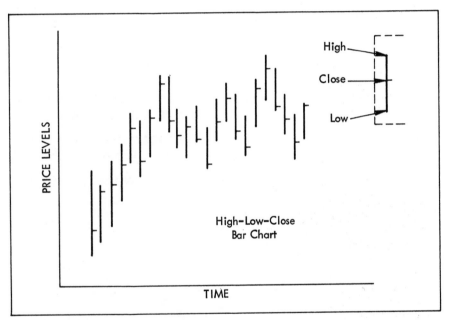

Illustration B-2

See: *Daily High-Low Chart*
P & F/Point and Figure Chart

Barter   To trade goods directly, without a medium of exchange, such as money.

Example: An accountant offers a given number of hours of services for an adding machine.

Basic Commodities   Commodities defined by law of the U.S. government as basic and thereby qualifying to be price supported or eligible for preferred loans or payments.

Examples:
Corn, wheat, cotton

Also known as: *Subsidized Commodities*

Basis

The difference between the futures price for a given commodity and the spot or cash price.

Example:

Soybeans	
Spot	$5.20
Futures	5.50
Basis = 5.50 − 5.20	
Basis = .30 future premium	

Basis is positive if the cash price is over the corresponding futures price, negative if under.

The difference can be due to a number of factors such as supply and demand of the commodity and/or substitute or storage and/or transportation problems.

Sometimes used to denote the difference in price between the various futures contract months.

Example:

Soybeans	
July	$5.50
September	5.40
Basis =	.10

Also used to indicate the difference between cash prices at a given location as opposed to current delivery point (location) prices.

In foreign exchange markets, basis is the difference between the Eurorates of two currencies, reflected as a forward discount or premium.

The following formula is used to determine the basis:

$$\text{Basis} = \frac{\text{spot} \times (\text{Eurodollar} - \text{Eurocurrency})}{100} \times \frac{\text{number of days to maturity}}{360 \text{ or } 365 \text{ (days)}}$$
(depending on currency)

Example:

Trade Date	March 15
Delivery Date	June 15
Eurocurrency Rates	
Dollar	19⅜% bid
Pound	17⅞% offer
Spot British Pound	2.1725

$$\text{Basis} = \frac{2.1725 \, (19.375 - 17.875)}{100} \times \frac{91}{365}$$

$$\text{Basis} = \frac{296.54625}{36500}$$

Basis = .0081 premium or $202.50/contract (25,000)

Note: Deutsche marks, Guilders, French francs, Swiss francs, Japanese yen, and Mexican pesos use 360 days for calculations. The British pound and Canadian dollar use 365 days for calculations.

Basis Chart

An analysis chart of the price pattern of the average monthly basis (cash versus futures difference) of a given commodity. The same general pattern is repeated yearly. See Illustration B-3.

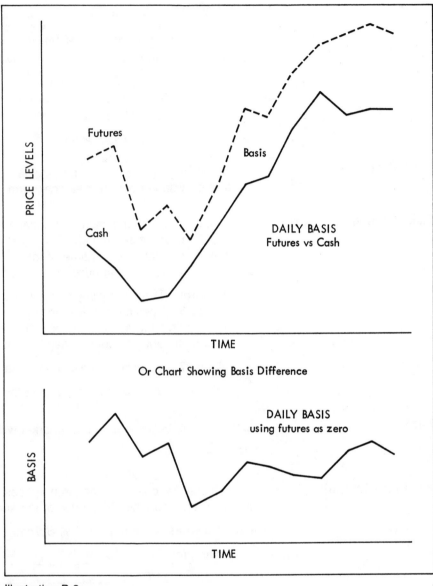

Illustration B-3

Basis Grade

The specific or standard quality of a commodity named and considered as the deliverable in an exchange's futures contract.

Also known as: *Contract Grade, Deliverable Grade, Deliverable Name, Sample Grade, or Par*

Example:
No. 1 Yellow Corn receives a premium
No. 2 Yellow Corn is at contract price (basis grade)
No. 3 Yellow Corn receives a discount

Note: Other factors such as weight, moisture content, damage, etc., determine acceptability and ultimate discount or premium.

Basis Point

The smallest increment or gradation of price movement possible in trading a given contract.

Also known as: *Minimum Price Fluctuation, Point, Tick*

Example:

Commodity	Basis Point Minimum Fluctuation	Dollar Value
Wheat	1/4 per bushel	$12.50
Ginnie Mae	1/32 of a dollar	31.25
Gold	10¢ per ounce	10.00
Cattle	2¹/₂¢ per pound	10.00
Sugar #11	1/100¢ per pound	11.20

See: *Maximum Price Fluctuation*

Basis Risk

The hazard arising when the difference between the actuals and futures price narrows or widens from the historical norm over the life of the contract.

Basis Trading

The buying or selling of a cash contract at a given number of points above or below that in the futures market. The purchase or sale may be immediate, with the price established at time of trade; or deferred at the agreed upon basis, with the actual cash price established later.

Example: The nearby soybean futures contract is November and trading at 6.40 per bushel. Depending on the availability of supplies the cash merchant may or may not be willing to acquire or sell inventory. The merchant's action for cash transactions might be the following:

Bid 6.37 per bushel. 3 basis under the November futures.

Offer 6.44 per bushel. 4 basis over the November futures.

Bear

Someone who believes the prices/market will decline.

See: *Bull*

Bear Call (Spread)

Two call options, paired for margin purposes, in which the strike price of the long is greater than the strike price of the short.

Also known as: *Vertical Bear Call Spread*

Example:

Option	Strike
Long 1 Dec T-bond Call	@ 60
Short 1 Dec T-bond Call	@ 58

See: *Bear Put Spread/Vertical Bear Put Spread*
Bull Call Spread/Vertical Bull Put Spread
Bull Put Spread/Vertical Bull Put Spread

Bear Market

A market where prices are declining, indicating a downward trend. This trend is based on long-term (months or years) decline.

See: *Bull Market*

Bear Put (Spread)

Two put options, paired for margin purposes, in which the strike price of the short is greater than the strike price of the long.

Also known as: *Vertical Bear Put Spread*

Example:

Option	Strike
Long 1 Dec T-bond Put	@ 66
Short 1 Dec T-bond Put	@ 68

See: *Bear Call Spread/Vertical Bear Call Spread*
Bull Call Spread/Vertical Bull Call Spread
Bull Put Spread/Vertical Bull Put Spread

Bear Raid

Strong short selling by a group of bears, with no fundamental justification except to force the market down in order to profit by buying to cover short sales at lower prices.

Bgt

A standard abbreviation for *bought*.

See: *Buy/BOT*

Bid

A proposal at a given time on the floor of an exchange to buy a specific quantity of a commodity at a specific price.

See: *Asked/Offer*

Bid and Ask

The highest price declared (wanted) by a buyer at a given time and the lowest price declared (offered) by a seller quoted at the same time.

Also known as: *Quotation or Quote*

Bill

A formal, written document specifying conditions of commerce.

See: *Bill of Exchange*
Bill of Lading
Bill of Sale

A document listing expenses or showing accounting, inventory, and customer billing information for actual commodities being received or delivered. Bills may represent original details or adjustments and cancellations.

Also known as: *Invoice*

Bill of Exchange

A written order by one party instructing a second party to pay (on demand or at a specified time in the future) a specific amount of money to a third party. The bill of exchange extends credit and secures payment and is generally in the form of a check.

Also known as: *Draft*

Bill of Lading

An in-transit document issued by the transportation company acknowledging goods received for transportation. This bill serves as both receipt and contract to transport. A bill of lading may be either negotiable ("to order") or nonnegotiable ("straight"), which specifies the receiver. If negotiable, this document serves as an instrument of ownership and can be bought, sold or traded.

Also known as: *B/L and Blading*

See: *Clean Bill of Lading*
Inland Bill of Lading
On-Board Bill of Lading

Bill of Sale

The document that passes title from seller to buyer.

Blackboard Trading	An old method of trading in which buyers and sellers make bids and offers on a slate board. Trades posted as the bid or offer are accepted (executed).
	Sometimes referred to simply as *Board Trading*.
	See: *Auction*
B/L, Blading	**See:** *Bill of Lading*
Blank Endorsement	A negotiable instrument, signed by an endorser, that conveys title but is not signed over to a specified party. A blank endorsement is payable to bearer.
	Also known as: *Endorsement in Blank*
	See: *Endorsement*
Blanket Policy	A closed insurance contract in which the insured pays in advance a lump sum based on an estimate of protection for the term of the policy. Actual contents are not specified; coverage is for any or all items in the facility.
	See: *Floating Policy/Open Policy* *Special Risk Policy*
Blocked Exchange	A government policy that permits only specified foreign exchange (currency) transactions.
Blotter	A daily record of transactions.
	See: *Trade Blotter*
Board (Governing)	A group of commercial leaders chosen or elected as exchange officials responsible for fair conduct of business and the rules and regulations of the exchange.
Board Trading	**See:** *Blackboard Trading*
Book Transfer	A transfer of title without physically delivering the product.
Booth	A location on the floor of the exchange equipped with telephones to receive orders. The space is generally a small (2 ft × 3 ft), semi-enclosed cubicle.
Bonded Warehouse	A warehouse licensed by the government and authorized to hold taxable goods pending the payment of custom duties and taxes.
BOT	A standard abbreviation for bought.
	See: *Buy/Bgt*
Box Spread	Four option positions paired for margin purposes. A box spread is a granted put option matched with a long call at the same exercise price, then coupled with a granted call and a long put, at another common strike price. Depending upon the exchange, the expiration month must be the same or may be different for both sets of pairs.

Example:

Option	Strike
Short 1 Mar Gold Put	@ 380
Long 1 Mar Gold Call	@ 380
Short 1 Mar Gold Call	@ 400
Long 1 Mar Gold Put	@ 400

Bona Fide
Carried out in good faith; considered authentic or within guidelines, rules, or laws.

Bracketing
The dividing of a trading session into equal time segments and coding of each segment with a symbol or code. The code is used to verify time of an execution of trade and submission to the clearing house.

Example:

Chicago Board of Trade	
7:30–8:00	$
8:00–8:30	A
8:30–9:00	B
9:00–9:30	C

Branch
Any office of a brokerage organization other than the main or home office.

Break
A rapid, sharp decline in price resulting from unexpected news.

See: *Break-Out*
Bulge

The inability of two brokers to match their buy and sell executions on the floor of the exchange.

The inability of a broker to match buy and sell transactions to the clearing house.

Also known as: *Unmatched Trade(s)*

Breakaway Gap
A significant space between price ranges that follows a period of narrow trading and may indicate a sharp future movement. See Illustration B-4.

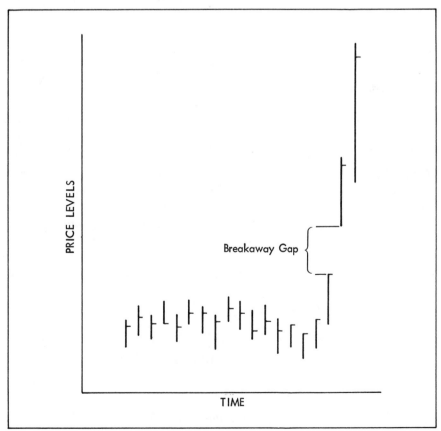

Illustration B-4

See: *Gap*
Common Gap
Exhaustion Gap
Runaway Gap

Break-out

A very sharp movement in price from the prevailing price level. See Illustration B-5.

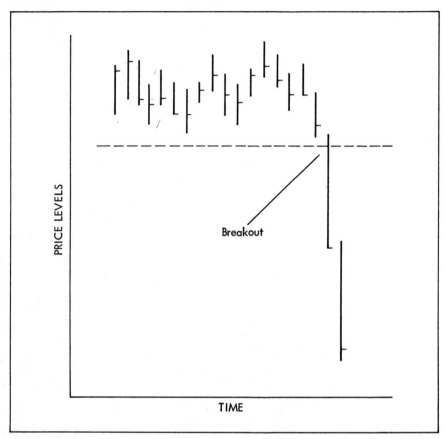

Illustration B-5

See: *Break*
Bulge

Break Sheet

A document used in an operations department to check unmatched trades. One type of break sheet is prepared by the clearing house and lists trades that do not match submissions from a brokerage house or a floor broker. A second type is prepared by the broker based on discrepancies between the firm's books and a clearing house report.

Broker

An agent who executes buy and/or sell orders and is paid a commission or fee.

See: *Trader*
Carrying Broker
Executing Broker/Floor Broker/Pit Trader
Two-Dollar Broker

A middleman between buyer and seller.

Brokerage

Fees paid to a broker for executing buy/sell transactions.

A business operated by a broker(s).

A detailed accounting bill prepared by a broker as an invoice.

Broker Number

A number assigned by an exchange to an eligible broker. This number is used in lieu of names between traders to identify the party being traded with.

An identifier assigned to its brokers by a firm to control commissions and accountings to the firm.

Bucketing

The illegal practice of soliciting and accepting orders but not executing them on a recognized exchange. The solicitor assumes the opposite side of the trade, gambling that customer purchase prices will decline or sell prices will advance.

Bulge

A rapid, usually temporary, increase in price. See Illustration B-6.

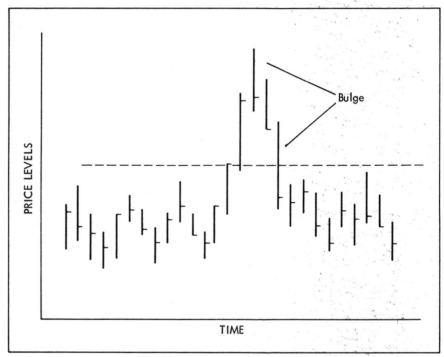

Illustration B-6

See: *Break*
   Break-out

Bull

Someone who believes prices or the market will rise.

See: *Bear*

Bull Call Spread

Two call options paired for margin purposes in which the strike price of the short is greater than the strike price of the long.

Also known as: *Vertical Bull Spread*

Example:

Option	Strike
Long 1 Dec T-bond Call	@ 58
Short 1 Dec T-bond Call	@ 60

See: *Bull Put Spread /Vertical Bull Put Spread*
   Bear Call Spread/Vertical Bear Call Spread
   Bear Put Spread/Vertical Bear Put Spread

Bullion

A precious metal, such as gold or silver, in a form other than coins, available for fabricating.

> **Example:**
> Bars
> Ingots
> Nuggets

Bullion Value

The value of bullion content of a coin at current market value.

Bull Market

A market where prices are advancing, indicating an upward trend. This trend is based on long-term (months or years) advance.

See: *Bear Market*

Bull Put (Spread)

Two put options, paired for margin purposes, in which the strike price of the long is greater than the strike price of the short.

Also known as: *Vertical Bull Put (Spread)*

> **Example:**
>
> | Option | Strike |
> |---|---|
> | Long 1 Dec T-bond Put | @ 68 |
> | Short 1 Dec T-bond Put | @ 66 |

See: *Bull Call Spread/Vertical Bull Call Spread*
Bear Call Spread/Vertical Bear Call Spread
Bear Put Spread/Vertical Bear Put Spread

Butterfly Spread

Four contracts (three separate positions), paired for margin purposes, that in diagram form (see below) resemble a triangle or butterfly wings.

For futures, a butterfly spread is positions of the same commodity in which two contracts (one position long or short) are in a common month and are balanced by two other positions (shorts or longs), one in an earlier month and the other in a later month.

> **Example:**
>
> Long 1 COMEX Gold Mar @ 360
> Short 2 COMEX Gold May @ 370
> Long 1 COMEX Gold July @ 385

Trade Price	MARCH	MAY	JULY
355			
360	L(1)		
365	Wing	Vertex	
370		S(2)	
375		Wing	
380			
385			L(1)
390			

For options, a butterfly spread is four options (three separate positions) of the same commodity and class in which two (longs or shorts) have a common strike price and are balanced by the other two (shorts or longs) of differing strike prices, one higher than the common strike price and one lower. Depending on exchange, expiration month must be the same or may be different for all positions in the spread.

Example:

Option	Strike
Long 1 Composit Index Call	@ 94
Short 2 Composit Index Call	@ 96
Long 1 Composit Index Call	@ 98

A butterfly diagram for options would look the same as the one for futures, but the points would reflect strike prices, not trade prices.

Buy

A purchase transaction.

The standard abbreviations *Bgt* and *BOT* are used to indicate bought or buy.

A long market position resulting from the purchase transaction.

Also known as: *Long*

See: *Sale*
Sell/Short

Buyer

The purchaser or holder of a long contract.

Also known as: *Purchaser*

In London the term *taker* is used.

See: *Grantor/Seller/Writer*

Buyer's Call

The granted right given to a buyer to establish a cash price at an agreed number of points (basis) above or below the contract price of a predetermined futures month. The buyer is also granted a certain period of time within which to fix the cash price by purchasing the futures contract for the seller's account.

Example: On December 1, a copper dealer has copper inventory and is hedged in the futures market with a March contract short at 67.00. A manufacturer requires raw materials during the month of March but does not wish to fix a cash commitment this far forward at this time.

The manufacturer enters into an agreement with the dealer to pay 50¢ over the futures market with the right to fix the price anytime within the next 60 days.

Futures Market	
Dec 1	Mar Copper @ 67.00
Dec 15	Mar Copper @ 66.00
Jan 2	Mar Copper @ 65.00

On January 2 the market has reacted as expected, and the buyer fixes the cash price at 65.50, or .50 above the market, and establishes a futures contract for the dealer at 65.00.

Note: The above transaction moves the cash copper from the dealer to the manufacturer at 65.50 and provides a long futures to the dealer at 65.00, thereby liquidating the short March Copper futures contract at 67.00.

See: *On Call*
Seller's Call

Buyer's Market

A market with heavy offerings; supply exceeds demand, there are more sellers than buyers, and prices are reduced.

See: *Seller's Market*

Buy-in

A type of purchase transaction used to cover or offset a short position. A buy-in may be used by a broker to close out an account that has failed to raise necessary margin.

Also known as: *(Short) Cover*

See: *Liquidation*
    Close-out/Offset

Sometimes used to refer to the creation of a new long position.

Buying Hedge

The purchase of contracts to protect against price increases.

Example: In March, a processor knows he/she will require wheat in July. On March 1, the *cash market* is selling @ 5.40 per bushel. The processor wants to fix the forward July purchase price at current market level. At the same time, the following transaction is made:

Futures	Buy 5M July Wheat 5.44

Should the market advance between March and July,

	March		July		Results
Cash Price	5.40	Buy	5.73		5.73 purchased
Futures	5.44	Sell	5.77	−	.33 gain
					5.40 net cost

Should the market decline,

	March		July		Results
Cash Price	5.40	Buy	5.06		5.06 purchased
Futures	5.44	Sell	5.10		+.34 loss
					5.40 net cost

The transactions net out to the 5.40 price fixed in March, four months before the physical need occurs. The futures gain is deducted from the final price paid or, if a loss, added to the final price paid. The hedger saved the cost of storage and financing.

Note: The hedger has the option of receiving the wheat via the futures position or in the cash market.

See: *Selling Hedge*

Buying Power

Equity exceeding the requirement in an account. This amount can be used for additional purchases or be paid out to the clients.

Buying Power = Equity − Requirement Level

Example:

Account XYZ	
Requirements	$10,000
Maintenance	7,500
Equity	12,450
Buying power	2,450

Also known as: *Excess*

Buy on Close

An instruction to buy a contract at the end of the day's trading at the best possible price (at or near closing price).

Example:

Buy 5000 Sept Soybeans on the close

may also be written as

B 5M U BNS OC

The above order can be executed only during the exchange-specified closing period. Any price traded within the range for this period is acceptable. The order is not guaranteed the best price or last posted price of the range. If the order has a price limit, then the execution can be only that price or better while still within the closing range.

See: *Sell on Close*

Buy on Open

An instruction to buy a contract at the beginning of the day's trading at the best possible price (at or near opening price).

Example:

Buy 1 Oct Soybean oil on the open

may also be written as

B 1 V SBO Opening Only

This order can be executed only during the exchange-specified opening period. Any price within the trading range is acceptable. The best price of the range or first price posted cannot be guaranteed. If the order has a price limit, then the execution must be at that price or better while still within the opening range.

See: *Sell on Open*

Byproducts

Products generated from the same raw materials.

Example: Soybean oil and soybean meal from soybeans

Also known as: *Complementary Products*

CAD (COD)

The standard abbreviation for *Cash on (at) Delivery*. CAD describes a condition or term in an agreement regarding the method of payment for a commodity.

Call

An exchange-traded option contract that gives the purchaser the right, but not the obligation, to enter into an underlying futures contract to buy a commodity at a stated strike price any time prior to the option's expiration date. The grantor of the call has the obligation, upon exercise, to deliver the long futures.

Example:
The buyer (traded)

Option	Strike Price	Expire Date	Trade Price
October 12: Long 1 Mar Sugar #11	@ 1200	March 9	1.20

During the dates of October 12 and March 9 of the next year, the March futures market trades at 1400.

The buyer exercises the right to be long (the futures) at 1200 (option strike price):

Futures	Long	1	Mar Sugar #11		@ 1200
Market			Mar Sugar #11		@ 1400
(transaction)				Points +	200 gain
Buyer paid option premium:				Points −	120
				Net Points	80 gain

(Less commission and fees upon ultimate sale of the futures.)

When the buyer receives the long, the seller of the option receives a short futures at 1200:

Futures	Short	1	Mar Sugar #11	@ 1200	
Market			Mar Sugar #11	@ 1400	
(transaction)			Points	−	200 loss
Seller received option premium				+	120 gain
			Net Points		80 loss

(Less commissions and fees upon ultimate closeout of the futures.)

An option that entitles the purchaser to buy the actual commodity at a specified price within a stipulated time.

See: *Put*

Call (Margin)

See: *Margin Call*

Call (On)

See: *On Call*
Buyer's Call
Seller's Call

Call (Opening/Closing)

The period of time, designated by the given exchange, during which trade is conducted to establish the opening or closing price levels for each contract month.

Cancel Former Order

An order that cancels a previous order by replacing it with "changes," thereby establishing a new order. The standard abbreviation is *CFO*.

Example:
On November 5, 10:05 a.m., a trader places an order:

Buy 1 Mar Gold @ 380.00

On November 5, 11:30 a.m., the same trader places the order:

Buy 1 Mar Gold @ 385.00 cancel former order 380.00

The order placed at 10:05 a.m. is automatically cancelled, leaving the order, placed at 11:30 a.m., as the current order.

This designation may not be used to change part of an order.

Cancellation

The termination of an unexecuted order with the broker.

The termination of a position prior to fulfillment (delivery), exercise, assignment, or liquidation.

Note: The trade is not terminated but removed from the client's account. The trade either belonged to another client or is a trading error to the broker. No trade may be terminated by cancellation once it has been cleared through the clearing house.

C & F

The standard abbreviation for *Cost and Freight*, a term used in an actual commodity agreement.

Example: This term includes transportation, demurrage at sight, insurance, loading or unloading, enroute care (icing, heating, ventilating), storage, etc.

Capital Gains

Profits realized from the sale of capital assets. Under federal tax law, capital gains may be either short term and taxed at an individual's full income-tax rate or long term and taxed at a lower rate.

Capital Requirement	A minimum financial standard (determined by an authorized exchange, the National Futures Association, or the Commodity Futures Trading Commission) required of a futures commission merchant.
Car	A term describing the vehicle used to transport a contract, such as "a car of lumber." This term is related to railroad-car capacity. Also, loosely used interchangeably when referring to a contract or lot that may not equal a rail car capacity or actual use of a rail car for transporting.
Carrier's Certificate	An import document certifying details of shipment, ownership, port of lading, etc. **Also known as:** *Carrier's Certificate and Release Order*
Carrying Broker	The clearing member of an exchange who "holds" the position(s) and maintains the accounting of the position(s) for a nonclearing member and other clearing members. **See:** *Broker* *Executing/Floor Broker/Pit Trader* *Floor Trader/Market Maker* *Two-Dollar Broker*
Carrying Charges	The cost of financing or all costs for warehousing an actual commodity, including insurance, interest charges, estimated loss (gain) in weight and freight. **Note:** In a full carrying-charge market, price differences in the futures market between delivery months reflect full carrying charges. In the delivery against the futures, this cost includes all charges of taking delivery in a given month, prepaid allowances, inspections, and brokerage. **Example:** These charges include weighing, sampling, checking weights, labor costs, and storage charges.
Cartel	An international syndicate the purpose of which is monopolistic control of a particular market. **Example:** OPEC (Organization of Petroleum Exporting Countries).
Cash Balance	The actual cash or status of cash being shown in an account at a given time. This amount can be either a credit or a debit.
Cash Commodity	**See:** *Actual(s)*
Cash Commodity for Futures	**See:** *AA/Against Actuals*
Cash Delivery Account	A customer account created to reflect the flow of physical commodity movement. **Note:** A cash delivery account is always a nonregulated account.
Cash Forward	The transaction in which a cash dealer sells an actual commodity for delivery at a specified date in the future. Forward time is not limited but generally is fairly short.

Example: On March 13 an owner (holder) of an actual commodity sells a specified quantity to a buyer on the basis of delivery and settlement to take place on March 16. No cash or product changes hands until the future, agreed-to date.

Cash Market

The market in which purchase and sale transactions for immediate delivery of the actual commodity are made.

This market may be the cash section of a futures exchange or, for the live-stock industry, for example, the stockyard.

Also known as: *Spot Market*

Note: The term *spot* may also refer to a futures contract of the current month that is still active as a "futures" but may be deliverable immediately or within the current month.

See: *Forward Market*
Futures Market

Cash Price

The sale-price quotation or current offering for a commodity in the cash market.

Also known as: *Spot Price*

Cash Settlement

A finalizing mechanism in which a contract is satisfied with a cash value calculation.

Cash may be given in lieu of the actual commodity, or it may be required in addition to physical delivery of a commodity (for example, when commodity quality necessitates a premium or a discount).

In finalizing a financial product, such as an index or foreign-exchange product, cash settlement is necessary because the contract represents a value rather than a physical product.

CEA

The standard abbreviation for the *Commodity Exchange Act*, the U.S. federal law that regulates the commodity contract markets.

Also, the standard abbreviation for the *Commodity Exchange Authority*, a regulatory agency created by the U.S. federal government empowered to administer the Commodity Exchange Act of 1936, before the establishment of the Commodity Futures Trading Commission in 1974.

Central Bank

An official organization authorized to issue national currency and regulate money and credit.

Certificate of Origin

An export document used to inform a buying country what country the goods were produced in.

CFO

See: *Cancel Former Order*

CFTC

The standard abbreviation for the *Commodity Futures Trading Commission*, the federal regulatory agency for the domestic futures traded on commodity markets.

See: *SEC/Securities Exchange Commission*

Changer

A member of an exchange who functions as an arbitrageur under special permission granted by that member's exchange. The changer offers an alternate means for fellow members to take advantage of price differentials that occur between their market and competing markets of the same commodity on another exchange.

> **Example:** The May Wheat contract at the Mid-America Exchange is suddenly selling at a premium over the similar contract at the Chicago Board of Trade. The Mid-America member is short the local market and wishes to take advantage of the discount without participating directly in the Board of Trade market.
>
> The trader approaches the changer as a buyer of May Wheat (Mid-America). The changer makes an offer based on what the changer can purchase Chicago May Wheat plus a service fee.
>
> If the trader and the changer agree, the following transactions take place:
>
> 1. The trader buys 5M May Mid Am Wheat
> 2. The changer sells 5M May Mid Am Wheat
> 3. The changer buys 5M May CBT Wheat
>
> By the willingness of the changer to arbitrage the two markets, the trader being serviced is able to liquidate the short position at a better price than the current local market place offered.

Note: The quantity of the trade must be equal. Since the Chicago Board of Trade contract which is a minimum of 5,000 bushels, the Mid-America trader must purchase 5 mini contracts in the Mid-America market.

Changer Fee

A service charge given to a changer for providing the function of a change transaction.

See: *Changer*

Changing

A mechanism whereby a member of one exchange is granted privileges to have a buy or sell for a given commodity executed on the floor of another exchange. Changing provides liquidity, keeps prices in line, and enables an exchange to better service its customers.

Charting

The graphical representation of numerical data, such as price and/or volume, for visual analysis. See Illustration C-1.

MOST COMMONLY USED GRAPHICS

PRICE LEVELS

```
                    X
                    5X
                    XX
                  X  XX
                  XXXX
                  XXXX
                  0 0 0
                  XX
                  XX
                  XX
                  X
```

Vertical Bar   Point and Figure

Chart Pictures	Price movement patterns, which, based on historical precedence, indicate a trend advance or decline and/or the extent of the trend. This tool is used by analysts who employ charting. See Illustration C-2.

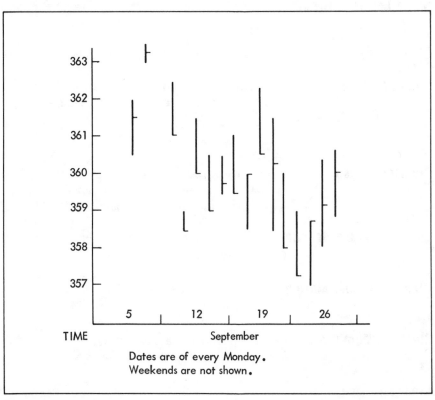

Illustration C-2

Check Slip	A confirmation of trades between members on the floor of an exchange.
Churning	Continuous buying and/or selling by a floor broker to create an appearance of volume. Excessive trading aimed at generating commissions at a customer's expense. (Small profits may equal or barely equal commissions.)
CIF	The standard abbreviation for *Cost Insurance and Freight*, which is paid to the port of destination. This term is used in an actual commodity agreement.
Claimant	The party making a claim for any purpose, such as an insurance claim or request for arbitration. **See:** *Arbitrator* *Respondent*
Class	A designation of option category, put or call of the same underlying futures contract.
Clean Bill	A sight or time draft with no other document attached. The term *clean bill* is also sometimes used when only nonnegotiable documents are attached. **See:** *Documentary Draft*
Clean Bill of Exchange	An undocumented bill; one not accompanied by any other document, such as a bill of lading.

Clean Bill of Lading	A document issued when the shipment is received in good order. This document has no qualifying language and indicates no damages or shortages.
Clean Letter of Credit	An instrument that does not require a document, such as a bill of lading, as condition for acceptance by a bank.
Clearing Fee	A sum charged by a clearing house for clearing trades through its facilities.
Clearing Fines	Charges levied on clearing members for lateness, errors, or omissions on clearing sheets or transfer sheets.
	Note: Members are also given reprimands for infractions of clearing house rules.
Clearing House	An exchange-associated, usually independent entity through which contracts are registered, settled, guaranteed, offset, and/or fulfilled through delivery of the commodity. Financial settlement is made through this organization.
Clearing House Account	A firm's general ledger account recording cash flow to and from the clearing house.
Clearing House Margin	The good-faith deposit made by a broker to the clearing house on open positions.
Clearing Member	A member of a clearing house. All trades must be registered and eventually settled with a clearing member.
Clearing Price	The official price established by the exchange at the close of each trading day and used as the common denominator for the given day's market settlement of variation money and the next day's price limits. The futures clearing price is used to set option strike prices and determine in-the-money and out-of-the-money conditions.
	This term is sometimes used interchangeably with *Closing Price*.
	Also known as: *Settlement Price (of futures)*
	See: *Closing Price/Price Range*
Clearing Sheet	A daily accounting report created by the clearing house for each clearing member that holds a commitment or had activity in a commodity serviced by that clearing house. The report provides the daily accounting of prior positions, the day's trading, and money settlements.
Close (The)	A period of time at the end of a trading day during which the transactions taking place establish the closing price range.
Close-out	A finalizing transaction by which an equal quantity and opposite (buy or sell) transaction eliminates an open (sell or buy) position(s).
	Also known as: *Offset*
	See: *Cover/Buy-in* *Liquidation*
	This term is sometimes used when a broker closes out an account for which necessary margin has not been supplied.

Closing Price/Closing Range	The one or more prices transacted during the period of time at the end of the trading session. When there is only one price, it is generally used as the settlement price. When there is more than one or a range of prices, a point designated by the exchange is deemed the settlement price. **See:** *Clearing Price/Settlement Price* *Opening Price*
Closing Purchase Transaction	A buy transaction in which the holder of a short position liquidates that position. **Also known as:** *Offset Transaction*
Closing Sale Transaction	A sell transaction in which the holder of a long position liquidates that position. **Also known as:** *Offset Transaction*
Collateral	Property or securities of determinable value pledged by a borrower to protect a lender against nonpayment of a loan.
Commerce	Business or trade.
Commission	The basic fee charged a customer by a broker for a purchase or sale transaction. A commission may be a flat charge or a percentage.
Commission House	A firm that, for a fee, buys and sells commodity contracts for customer accounts.
Commitment	The total number of open futures contracts (buys *or* sells) of a given commodity neither offset by an opposite futures transaction nor fulfilled by delivery or receipt. **Note:** Only one side is counted (buys or sells). **Also known as:** *Open Interest* The unfilled obligation to accept or make delivery of a contract.
Commitment of Funds	The funds allocated a position; actual investment.
Commodity	An article of commerce or a product that can be used for commerce. In a narrow sense, products traded on an authorized commodity exchange. Types of commodities include agricultural products, metals, petroleum, foreign currencies, and financial instruments and indexes.
Commodity Credit Corporation	A corporation, wholly owned by the U.S. government, within the Department of Agriculture that is subject to the general supervision and direction of the Secretary of Agriculture. Its responsibilities are to maintain adequate supplies of agriculture commodities and their orderly distribution; to conduct price support, export and storage programs; and to engage in buying, selling and lending activities, as well as, foreign trade.
Commodity Exchange Act	**See:** *CEA*
Commodity Exchange Authority	**See:** *CEA*

Commodity Loan

The financing of commodity production, generally agricultural commodities. Lending institutions will make funds available for seed, fertilizer and hedge financing against the farmer's crop and/or other collateral. Lenders are heavily reliant on the futures markets in protecting their interests.

A federal program makes nonrecourse loans to farmers as a primary means of government price supporting operations. The farmer uses the crop as collateral. Redemption may be made by payment of the loan and interest or default by forfeiting the crop to the government thereby cancelling the loan and all interest charges.

Commodity Paper

Negotiable bills of exchange backed by the value of staple commodities, in freight cars aboard ship or warehouse and insured, and evidenced by shipping and/or storage bills or bills of lading.

Upon default, the lender may sell the commodity to cover loan and collection expenses.

Commodity Pool Operator

An individual or company who invests a pool of money on behalf of a group of people. A commodity pool operator must be registered with the Commodity Futures Trading Commission, as well as meet the qualifications and follow the regulations stated in the Commodity Exchange Act.

The standard abbreviations for this term are *CPO* or simply *Pool Operator*.

Example: The operator solicits equal amounts of funds from a number of investors. When the appropriate number of individuals have been sold (let's say 10), each contributes a given amount (let's say $5,000). The pool is formed as a separate entity representing the 10 parties and has a pooled cash value of $50,000 for trading use.

Commodity Price Index

A price index measuring average prices of a group of commodities.

Example: The prices of five commodities:

Copper	61.00
Sugar	8.00
Wheat	3.30
Lumber	57.00
Cattle	63.00
	192.30

Divide 5 (the number of commodities) into 192.30 (the total of the five prices), which equals 38.46. The index in this group is 38.46.

Note: This term is not to be confused with the product *Indexes*.

See: *Index*

Commodity Product Spread

The spreading of futures contracts consisting of a primary, raw commodity and its byproducts. The positions are different commodities, same exchange in the same crop year, if applicable.

Also known as: *Source Spread*

Example: Crush/Reverse Crush and Crack/Reverse Crack. A crush spread looks like this:

Long	5M	Aug Soybeans
Short	1	Aug Soybean Oil
Short	1	Aug Soybean Meal

Note: The unique characteristic of this spread is that it contains three positions, unlike the more common two-position spread.

Commodity Rate

A railroad freight rate applied to specific types of commodities for shipment between specified points.

Commodity Trading Advisor

An individual or company who offers advice, for profit (compensation), on the purchase or sale of a commodity. The trading advisor will normally submit customer-approved orders for execution. The commodity trading advisor must be registered with the Commodity Futures Trading Commission, as well as meet the qualifications and follow the regulations stated in the Commodity Exchange Act.

This term is also known by the standard abbreviation *CTA*.

This term is not to be confused with a commission house. Commodity trading advisors receive more than the usual commission charged by brokers for their expertise.

Common Gap

Two or more sequential price levels on a chart reflecting no trade activity. They can appear at any time but generally hold little significance. This event is illustrated by no trading at prices between the previous day's high or low and the next day's high or low. See Illustration C-3.

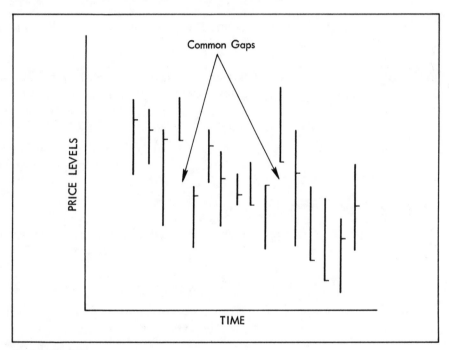

Illustration C-3

See: *Gap*
Breakaway Gap
Exhaustion Gap
Runaway Gap

Complementary Products

See: *Byproduct(s)*

Compliance

Action to "comply" with rules and/or regulations.

A division in a commodity department responsible for adherence to the rules and/or regulations of the exchanges, National Futures Association, or the Commodity Futures Trading Commission.

The compliance area at an exchange or clearing association is referred to as an audit department.

Conditional Endorsement

An endorsed instrument with additional wording that creates a condition that must be fulfilled before payment.

> **Example:** A sales contract may read payment due "upon delivery."

See: *Endorsement*

Confirmation

A notice of trade activity given to a client specifying the commodity bought (sold), quantity, and price.

> **Example:**

This is to confirm on
May 16 Bought 5 Mar Silver   @ 834.00
May 16 Sold 3   May Copper @ 61.00

The document usually contains a preprinted paragraph advising the client of the responsibility to notify the broker immediately if there is an error.

Note: Cash movements in and out of the account may be confirmed to the client on the same or a similar document.

Conflict of Interest

A contradiction between a person's other interests and his/her responsibilities in a position of trust.

Congestion

A market condition in which buyers and sellers have equal advantage, thereby preventing the market prices from moving out of a narrow range. Usually the ownership of commitments turns over many times while the market is in this state.

This term may sometimes be used in resistance areas. The market reaches a price level that finds willing sellers delaying further advance or willing buyers delaying further decline.

Congestion Area

On an analysis chart, a sideways price movement or one showing little fluctuation, indicating that old positions are being liquidated and new ones established easily within the given price range. See Illustration C-4.

See: *Support Areas*
Resistance Areas

Consignment

An actual commodity transferred or delivered to another party for sale or disposal.

Consolidation Pattern

On an analysis chart, a price pattern indicating an existing trend that pauses before continuing.

> **Example:**
> Flag and Pennant Patterns. See Illustration C-5.

Also known as: *Continuation Pattern*

See: *Reversal Pattern*

Containerization

The packing and shipping of goods in standard, large, rectangular metal units designed for bulk movement of multiple packages.

These containers are commonly used in rail, air, barge, steamship, and truck transportation.

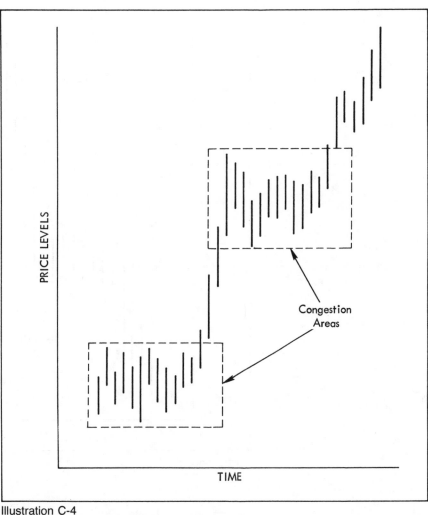

Illustration C-4

Contango

A market in which distant months sell at a premium over near months. See Illustration C-6.

Also known as: *Normal market, Carrying charge*

A basic pricing system that includes carrying charges rather than separate payments for insurance, warehousing, etc. A premium is paid to cover such charges for the more future months or later deliveries.

The practice of postponing delivery. The buyer pays for the privilege granted by the seller to extend time of delivery.

See: *Backwardation*

The cost factors used to calculate one period (point) to the future period (point).

Example: Carrying charges for gold carried for 3 months

Current Market Price	$380.00	per oz.
Interest 18% Annual	15.48	90 days
Storage .04¢ per Day per Bar	.036	90 days
3-Month Market Price	$395.516	per oz.
or		
March Gold	380.00	
April	385.10	
May	390.30	
June	395.50	

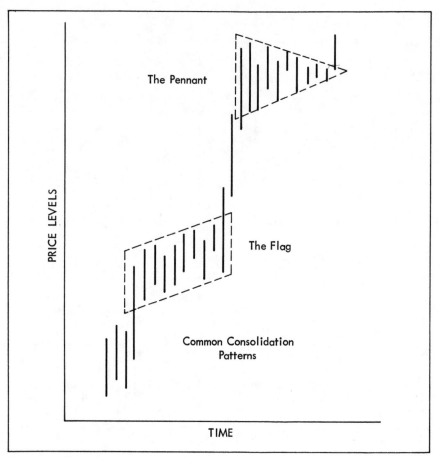

Illustration C-5

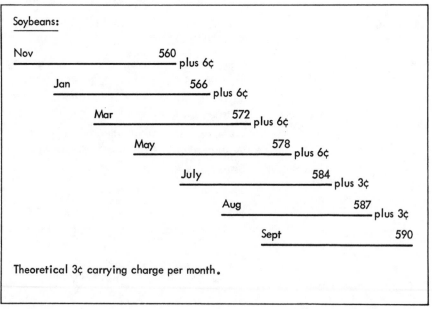

Illustration C-6

Contingency Order

A buy or sell order for a specified number of contracts in a specified commodity and month with additional limits on the nature of the trade. Limitations generally include price and/or time guidelines.

Sometimes action is to take place *if* something else occurs. These orders are designed for maximum control by the client.

Example:

Buy 5 July Platinum 392.00 limit off at 12:30 p.m.

may also be written as

B 5 N PLAT 39200 off 12:30

In this order the customer has placed a buy order to purchase at $392.00; but, if not executed by 12:30 p.m. of that day, the order is to be cancelled.

Buy 5 July Platinum 392.00 if
    Apr trades 387.00

may also be written as

B 5 N PLAT 39200 if J 38700

With this order the customer is willing to buy July at $392.00 if (contingent) April trades at $387.00. The broker has no order until April trades at $387.00.

See: *Market Order*

Continuation Pattern

See: *Consolidation Pattern*

Contract

A binding agreement between buyer and seller in a transaction.

See: *Futures Contract*
Forward Contract

This term is also used to indicate a unit of the commodity traded.

Example:

Grain	5,000	bushels
Copper	25,000	pounds
Gold	100	ounces

Contract Carrier

A transporter under contract to carry specific goods, as distinguished from a common carrier.

Contract Difference Account

A general ledger account created to receive all settlement collections, payments and purchase and sale (P & S) distributions reflecting one exchange or one commodity within one exchange. A contract difference account is a control account.

Contract Grade

See: *Basis Grade*

Contract Month

The calendar month a futures contract matures and becomes deliverable.

Also known as: *Delivery Month*

Example: Chicago Wheat is available for delivery only during the contract months: March, May, July, September, and December.

See: *Active Months*

Contract Month Symbol

Standard, acceptable abbreviations that identify the calendar month in a futures or options contract. These codes are also used on transmitting devices and trade tickets.

Example:

January "F", February "G", March "H"

Also known as: *Ticker Symbols*

Contract Price

The official price paid under the terms of the contract.

Also known as: *Term Price*

Control Account

An account that contains summary transactions that balance to detailed account transactions.

Example:

Contract difference account (general ledger)
Customer accounts (detail accounts)

Controlled Account

An account over which an individual or organization other than the holder exercises trading authority (control) to buy and sell without notification to the holder. Selection, timing, amount, and price are included in the authority.

Also known as: *Power-of-Attorney Account, Discretionary Account, or Managed Account*

See: *Guided Account*

Controlling Interest

A percentage of ownership that empowers the authorized holder to exercise governing direction of the entity.

Conversion

Three commodity positions combined for margin purposes. The positions must be long put, long futures, and short call. The delivery month must be the same for all three positions, and the strike price must be the same for the two option positions.

Example:

Option	Strike Price
Long 1 Dec T-bond Put	66
Short 1 Dec T-bond Call	66

Futures	Trade Price
Long 1 Dec T-bond	63 25/32

See: *Reverse Conversion*

An exchange for value between currencies.

Example:

U.S. Currency $1.00   =   200 pesetas
(approximate)

Note: Rates are in constant fluctuation.

The process of changing raw materials into finished product.

Example: Soybean conversion is into soybean meal and soybean oil.

Cooperative	A form of business organization for some aspect of production or consumption.
	Example: A group of farmers form a cooperative to pool use of equipment and finance borrowing for seed and fertilizer. In turn, they pool their produce when marketing.
	See: *Farm Cooperative*
Corner	The purchase or sale of a quantity that gives the trader control of the market and thereby of the price. To corner a market is illegal.
	Example: The visible supply of a given commodity is 100,000 units. A person or group of people agree to coordinate a systematic effort to own a controlling amount of the 100,000 units. Depending on the market distribution, the controlling amount could be as little as 10 percent or 50 or more percent. At the point where the buyer's presence influences market prices, a corner is assumed.
Corporate Account	An account in which the customer is a registered corporation rather than an individual. Such an account would always be in the name of the corporation and not in the name of any of the individuals associated with it.
	Note: This account is always a customer account to the brokerage firm that services this corporate client and as such is considered a segregated account for reporting purposes.
	See: *Customer Account*
	A proprietary account of the brokerage house. This account is used to carry inventory in the products the proprietor handles. This account has nothing to do with customer activity and is maintained as a firm's own trading account.
	Note: This account is considered a nonsegregated account for reporting purposes.
	Example: A stock firm trades financial instrument commodities to leverage and protect capital.
	See: *House Account*
Corporate Resolution	A declaration or amendment to the corporation bylaws reviewed and approved by the executive board of the corporation. To be fully executed, it must be signed and bear the corporate seal.
Cost and Freight	**See:** *C&F*
Cost, Insurance, and Freight	**See:** *CIF*
Cover	The close-out or offset of a previously established short position.
	Also known as: *Short Cover*
	See: *Liquidation/Buy-in* *Evening up*
	Security (in cash or another acceptable form) provided by a clearing member to a clearing house to cover original or variation obligations existing on contracts resulting from market activity.

41

Covered Option

A granted call option is matched, for margin purposes, with a long position in the underlying futures contract; or a granted put option is matched with a short position in the underlying futures contract.

Example:

Option	Strike Price
Short 1 July Sugar #11 Call	20.00

Futures	Trade Price
Long 1 July Sugar #11	22.00

This option is considered covered in that the long futures at 22.00 offsets any short futures entering the account as a result of an assignment:

Option:
Assignment of call results in Short @ 20.00
Futures in account   Long @ 22.00

The result is no further exposure on the futures position.

Option	Strike Price
Short 1 July Sugar #11 Put	23.00

Futures	Trade Price
Short 1 July Sugar #11	22.00

The seller of the put is selling the right for the buyer to be short. Therefore, the seller, when assigned, receives a long.

Option:
Assignment of Put Results   Long @   23.00
Futures in Account   Short @   22.00

The result is no further exposure on the futures position.

Covered Position

Any position matched with another offsetting position for hedging or margin purposes.

Example:

Long 1   COMEX   Gold   Apr   390.00
Short 1   COMEX   Gold   Aug   400.00

CPO

See: *Commodity Pool Operator*

Crack Spread

The buying of crude oil while taking the reverse action in refinery products. Any combination of energy futures may be used, provided that the number of crude contracts equals the number of product contracts.

Example:

Long 3 Dec Crude Oil
Short 2 Dec Gasoline
Short 1 Dec Heating Oil

Long 1 Mar Crude Oil
Short 1 Mar Heating Oil

See: *Commodity Product Spread*
Reverse Crack Spread
Summer Crack Spread
Winter Spread

Credit

The ability to obtain goods (services) on a promise to pay later.

Elimination of a liability or creation of an asset.

Credit Balance

An excess of credits over debits; funds on deposit.

See: *Debit Balance*

Credit Limit

The maximum amount of credit approved for a given entity.

Credit Line

An overdraft privilege that grants loans to a customer without separate approvals.

> **Example:** granting a loan on issued checks with no available funds on deposit.

Also known as: *Line of Credit*

Credit Spread

Any option/option spread which results in a net collect value.

> **Example:**
>
> | Option | Premium |
> |---|---|
> | Sold: | |
> | 1 July Sugar #11 Call 20 @ 3.05 | $3,416.00 cr |
> | Bought: | |
> | 1 Oct Sugar #11 Call 18 @ 1.75 | 1,940.00 dr |
> | Net Collect | $1,456.00 cr |

Note: Premium is received for the sell; premium is paid for the buy.

See: *Debit Spread*

Crop Insurance

Insurance provided to farmers by the Federal Crop Insurance Corporation, an agency of the Department of Agriculture, for unavoidable crop loss due to such causes as weather, insects, or disease.

Crop Production Adjustments

Limitations on farm production set by the Agricultural Stabilization and Conservation Service. Limitations include the amount of acreage allowable for certain crops, the amount of crops that can be sent to market, etc.

Crop Year

The calendar period for agricultural commodities to be planted and harvested.

> **Example:**
>
> | U.S. Wheat | from June 1 to May 31 |
> |---|---|
> | Cotton | from Aug 1 to July 31 |

Crop Year Break

The contract month that reflects the beginning of the new crop year.

> **Example:** A given commodity crop year is May of the current year to April of the next year. The crop year break is the first business day of May of the next year.

The period during which prices become solely influenced by the new crop as the old crop has ceased to be in existence. See Illustration C-7.

	Crop Year Break		
October	April/May		September
12 Month Period			

Illustration C-7

Cross Rate

A quote of an exchange rate by a third country. It is the reciprocal of the quote carried by a given country.

Example:

London dollar cross rate

How much of a third country currency one U.S. dollar will buy in London (pound sterling); the reciprocal of that in New York.

Deutsche mark   .4320   in New York

$$\text{A dollar cross rate in London} = \frac{1}{.4320} = 2.3148$$

Note: The rates are not always identical so arbitrageurs watch them closely for potential profits.

Cross Hedge

The practice of holding or controlling a cash position of a commodity different from the futures but still eligible as a bona fide hedge.

Example: A dealer in commercial paper requiring a hedge vehicle could use the CD (certificate of deposit) futures market. The only interest the dealer has with CD futures is the economic leverage the market can provide against the commercial paper product.

Cross Trading

The noncompetitive, simultaneous purchase and sale by a broker in the pit of an exchange for equal amounts of the same month of a contract at a single price. This matching must comply with Commodity Futures Trading Commission regulations.

Note: Other brokers may intervene and accept all or part of the amount that is bid and offered.

Example: A floor broker receives the following orders:

Buy 1 May Copper @ 6100 for customer A
Sell 1 May Copper @ 6100 for customer B

Market bidding is 6090; offering is 6110.

The broker enters the ring and may bid or offer at 6100 depending on what he/she believes is the most appropriate action for a rapid execution.

Assume the broker bid 6100 and no seller was found. Now the broker may offer 6100 while bidding at the same price, giving everyone present an opportunity to trade either or both sides of the market. If no one trades the bid or offer, the broker is permitted to trade between the two customers' orders at 6100.

Note: When lacking either order in the preceding example, the broker may assume the missing side to fill the order. The customer must authorize in writing the willingness to allow the broker to trade against the order.

Crush

The process that converts soybeans into soybean meal and soybean oil.

A spread between soybeans and soybean products. Soybean futures are bought and soybean oil and soybean meal futures are sold.

Also known as: *Paris Spread or Source Spread*

Example:

Long 5M Sept Soybeans
Short 1 Sept Soybean Meal
Short 1 Sept Soybean Oil

See: *Commodity Product Spread/Source Spread*
Reverse Crush Spread

CTA

See: *Commodity Trading Advisor*

Currency

A medium of exchange issued by the government; money in circulation. Paper money, coins, and Federal demand deposits (Treasury bills, notes, and the like).

Currency Swap

An exchange of currency made between two countries at an agreed-upon rate in order to stabilize international currency values.

Current Delivery Month

The most current calendar month in which a futures contract becomes due and is deliverable.

Also known as: *Spot Month*

Example: A given commodity has active months of March, May, July, and October. On February 10, March is the nearest trading month; so March is sometimes considered the spot month. In the strictest sense, however, this is not appropriate.

On March 1, March is the spot month, for deliveries can be made in this calendar month. Spot sometimes begins in the last days of the previous month if the contract specifications allow notices to be issued prior to the first calendar day.

Customer Account

Any individual or entity being serviced by an agent (broker) for a commission. Servicing generally includes advice, accounting, and order execution. The principals of the account cannot participate or have financial interest in the broker's business.

Note: A customer's account when trading domestic commodities must be segregated.

See: *Corporate Account/House Account*

Customer Agreement

A contract between brokerage firm and client outlining the criteria for handling the account. This document may or may not be required at the discretion of the handling firm.

Customer Margin

The rate of margin required by the exchange to be given to a futures commission merchant as a good-faith deposit against a commitment.

Also known as: *Speculator Margin*

Note: It is not uncommon for the commission house to require a greater deposit than the exchange amount.

See: *Hedge Margin*
House Margin

Customs Entries

Import documents required by U.S. customs for goods entering the country.

Examples: ID Entry/Immediate Delivery Entry
IT Entry/Immediate Transport Entry

Cyclic Analysis

Analysis that uses various seasonal factors as a basis to determine trends and prices.

> **Example:** See Illustration C-8. A long-term chart (20 years) on a given commodity shows prices reached peak levels in years 5, 10, 15, and 20. It also reflects extreme lows in years 3, 8, 13, and 18.

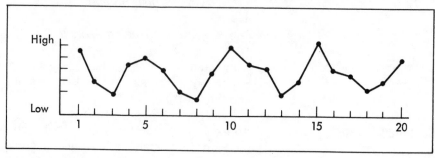

Illustration C-8

Analysis indicates that down markets extend for three years at a time and occur every five years. Therefore, on a historical basis, it might be reasonable to expect a down trend the next three years.

See: *Historical Analysis*
Fundamental Analysis
Technical Analysis

Daily High-Low Chart

A bar chart that displays daily highs, lows, and closes for a given period (day, week, month). This range chart is the simplest method of analysis. See Illustration D-1.

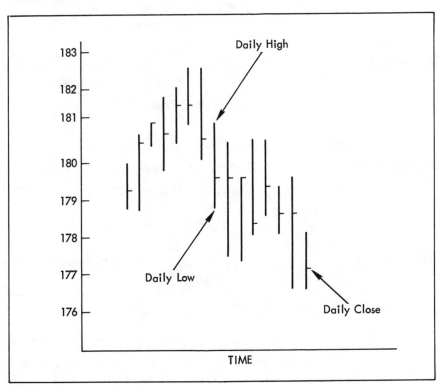

Illustration D-1

See: *Bar Chart*
   P & F/Point and Figure Chart

Daisy Chain
A series of trades or an intricate network of transactions generally not logically linked. This practice may be considered illegal when used to hide such activities as selling a price-controlled commodity at uncontrolled prices.

Day Order
An order with a price limit placed for execution during a given trading session; if not executed, it is automatically cancelled.

Also known as: *Straight Limit Order*

Example:

February 3	Sell 5M July Wheat 403

If the given price is not traded on February 3, the order is cancelled. Even if the price is traded on February 4, there would be no execution. A new order must be given.

Day Trade
The establishment and liquidation of the same position on the same trading day. An immediate profit or loss is established.

Also known as: *In-and-Out Trade*

Example:

(9 a.m.) May 2	Buy 1 Aug Gold @ 407.00
(2 p.m.) May 2	Sell 1 Aug Gold @ 409.00

A profit of $200, less commission, is made on the trade. Since the two trades offset each other, this liquidation takes priority over all other liquidations unless the customer instructs otherwise.

In London this practice is sometimes referred to as a *jobber trade*.

See: *Today's Trade/Top Day Trade*
Position Trading

Day Trader
An individual who both initiates and offsets trades in a single trading session to make quick profits on the market.

See: *Position Trader*
Scalper

Debit Balance
Amount due; a negative cash balance.

See: *Credit Balance*
Deficit
Unsecured

Debit Spread
Any option/option spread that results in a net pay value.

Example:

Option	Premium
Bought	
1 July Sugar #11 Call 20 @ 3.05	$3,416.00 dr
Sold	
1 Oct Sugar #11 Call 18 1.75	1,960.00 cr
Net pay	$1,456.00 dr

Note: Premium is paid for buy; premium is received for sell.

See: *Credit Spread*

Debt Instrument

An interest-bearing obligation.

Example:
Treasury Bills
Treasury Bonds
Corporate Bonds
Certificates of Deposit

Declaration Date

The date by which an option must be declared. If no declaration is made, the option is automatically abandoned on that date. (This term, generally used only for London options, corresponds to the term *expiration date* for U.S. domestic options.)

Date and time (generally 12:00 noon) for nontraded options are agreed to by grantor and holder.

Example:

2 lots of May Cocoa

Declaration Date   April 15   (12:00 noon)

Declaration or abandonment may take place any time up to 12:00 noon on April 15.

Date and time for traded options are officially determined by the rules of the exchange.

Declare

The statement of the intention to exercise or abandon an option (generally used only for London options).

Example:

	Call	*Purchase Date*	January 15
		Expiration Date	February 17

The holder of this call may declare his/her intentions to exercise or abandon to the clearing house anytime between the date of purchase (January 15) and the date of expiration (February 17).

Deep-Out-of-the Money

An option that has a strike price significantly out-of-the-money. In the case of a call, the strike price is higher than the underlying futures contract price; in the case of a put, the strike price is lower than the underlying futures contract price.

A deep-out-of-the-money condition exists when the underlying futures contract price movement increases the out-of-the-money status of the option. The various exchanges determine, for their own markets, the number of strike price intervals designation when an option is considered deep-out-of-the-money.

Example: An exchange rule states an option four or more strike levels from the current market is deep-out-of-the-money.

	Call Strike Price	*Futures Price*
Deep-out-of-the-money	470	
	460	
Out-of-the-money	450	
	440	
	430	
At-the-money	420	420
In-the-money	410	

Put Strike Price		Futures Price
In-the-money	470	
At-the-money	460	460
Out-of-the-money	450	
	440	
	430	
Deep-out-of-the-money	420	
	410	

Default

The failure of a holder of a short futures position to make physical delivery after the last delivery day. A penalty is charged to the failing short holder and given to the awaiting long holder.

Deferred Delivery Contract

A cash contract with delivery at some time in the future.

Example: On March 19 the price of copper is very attractive. A smelter needs 100 tons of copper 90 days from today.

Mar 19	Enters purchase agreement
June 19	Ore delivered and paid for

Note: The buyer may receive a discount or other considerations for prepayment.

Deferred Futures (delivery month)

The more distant months during which futures trading is taking place.

Also known as: *Distant Months*

Example: Assume that the current calendar month is March.

Spot	Near	Deferred
Mar	Apr	May thru Dec, Jan, and Feb

See: *Nearby (Delivery Month)*
Back Month

Deficit

Amount of liability.

The equity balance if the ledger balance and open positions liquidate negative.

Example:

April 13:				
Ledger Balance (Cash)				$500.00 cr
Open Positions				
Long	1	Oct COMEX Gold	@ 394.00	
		Settlement price	396.00	200.00 cr
Short	1	Dec COMEX Gold	@ 405.00	
Short	1	Dec COMEX Gold	@ 403.00	
		Settlement price	408.00	800.00 dr
Equity		(Deficit)		$100.00 dr

Notes:

Equity = Cash + Positions @ Market
Deficit = A negative equity

Margin requirements on open positions are not considered in determining liquidating deficit or credit balance.

Securities on deposit are not included in equity.

This term may also be used to indicate a negative equity and no open position.

See: *Debit Balance*
Excess
Unsecured

Deliverable Name/Grade

See: *Basis Grade*

Deliverable Supply

The available supply that has been certified by the exchange for possible delivery.

Example:

	(ounces)
All free Gold in N.Y. Vaults	2,000,000
Certificated Receipts	50,000

Notes:
In order to deliver over 50,000 ounces, the holders would have to get the metal certificated.

Deliverable supply is not visible supply.

Delivery

The changing of ownership (tender or receipt) or control of a physical commodity or cash equivalent.

Satisfaction of the futures contract under the specific terms and procedures established by the exchange.

Delivery Instructions

An export document giving specific instructions to an inland carrier concerning arrangements made to deliver the goods to a given pier or steamship line.

See: *Delivery Order*

A set of instructions from the buyer for acceptance of delivery of a commodity if not stipulated in the contract. Instructions may include where and/or how to deliver the goods.

Instructions from the receiver of a futures delivery notice to sell the contract and pass or reissue the notice of delivery to the next buyer.

Also known as: *Retender Instructions*

Delivery Month

See: *Contract Month*

Delivery Notice

Official, written notification stating the intentions of the holder of a short position to make delivery in satisfaction of or against a given futures contract.

Example: Contents of such a document might include issue date, name of issuer, notice price (settlement price of previous day), notice number, commodity, description of delivery (per respective exchange rules), total value to be paid, and endorsement of issuer.

Delivery Notice Issued

Action taken when a short contract holder elects to deliver the commodity to satisfy the short futures contract position.

This action is restricted to specified time periods determined by the individual exchanges and stated in their contract rules.

See: *Delivery Notice Stopped*

Delivery Notice Stopped

Action taken when a long futures contract holder receives notice of delivery and must take delivery of the commodity.

Note: The holding of the commodity may be for a short period of time, such as 24 hours, or indefinitely, as in actually using the commodity.

See: *Delivery Notice Issued*

Delivery Order

An import document, issued by a consignee to an initial carrier, authorizing release of cargo to a secondary carrier upon arrival.

Also known as: *Pier Release*

See: *Delivery Instructions*

Delivery Points

Locations and facilities designated by the exchange at which the physical commodity may be (stored and) delivered in fulfillment of a contract.

Example:

	Commodity	Delivery Points
NYMEX	#2 Heating Oil	Gulf Coast ex-shore facility having access to any Colonial Pipeline injection point
COMEX	Gold	NYC Borough of Manhattan licensed depository
CBT	Wheat	Regular warehouses in the Chicago switching district or the Burns Harbor switching district

Note: Delivery points may be more specific than city or pier location; a specific warehouse or terminal may be named.

Delivery Price

The actual price invoiced on the futures delivery. This price closes out the futures contract (both sides of the delivery). This price is determined and established by the settlement price of the previous close of business in the futures.

Example:

> *Original Purchase* May 10
> Bought 1 Oct COMEX Gold 394.00
>
> *Delivery* Oct 12
> Received 1 Oct COMEX Gold 400.00 T/N*

*Tender Notice

Note: The T/N trade at 400 assumes the opposite (offset) position for both the receiver and deliverer. The $600 difference between the original purchase price and the final delivery price is collected by the holder (profit) during the life of the contract. Conversely, the seller paid the difference (loss).

A quoted price that includes cost of shipping or a fixed price for delivery alone, within a specified area.

| **Delta Factor** | A percentage value of the amount that an option premium can be expected to change for a given unit change in the underlying futures contract. |

Delta Factor

A percentage value of the amount that an option premium can be expected to change for a given unit change in the underlying futures contract.

The factor takes into consideration the time remaining to an option's expiration, the volatility of the underlying futures contract, and the price relationship.

Example: Formula to calculate the delta factor for S & P 500 options:

Factors are available from all the clearing houses offering option trading. They change on a daily basis.

Demand Loan

A loan that has no fixed due date and is thereby payable on demand at any time.

Demurrage

The detention of a vessel, freight car, etc., beyond a specified departure time for waiting time, loading, or unloading.

The compensation for charges resulting from the delay for waiting time, loading, or unloading.

Depletable

Capable of being consumed by use or transformation; for example, oil or metals.

Depository

A person, place, or institution used for storing valuables.

Also known as: *Warehouse*

Depository Receipt

A document issued by a vault or warehouse and used in cash and futures transactions that guarantees the existence and availability of a given quantity and quality of a commodity held in storage at a given location. This instrument may be used to transfer ownership of the futures or actual commodity.

Also known as: *Warehouse Receipt*

See: *Negotiable Warehouse Receipt*
Nonnegotiable Warehouse Receipt

Depreciation

Decline in resale value in terms of use and/or purchasing power.

Example:

Condition	Value
A farmer purchases a tractor	$20,000
One year later sells	15,000
Depreciation	$ 5,000
Trade account buying power	$10,000
Next day (market value)	8,000
Depreciation (loss in buying power)	$ 2,000

Descending Triangle

A chart price pattern formed by price swings ending in lower high points so that the slope side of the triangle goes downward. See Illustration D-2.

See: *Ascending Triangle*
Pennant/Symmetrical Triangle

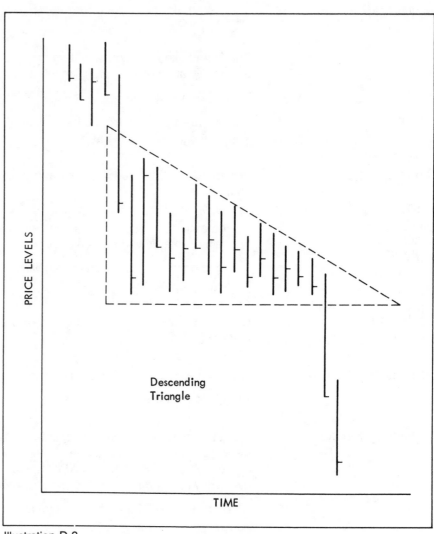

PRICE LEVELS

Descending
Triangle

TIME

Illustration D-2

Devaluation

A downward redefinition of the precious metal content in a country's currency or of one country's currency in relation to that of another country.

Example: A given currency's official rate of exchange to the U.S. dollar is 90¢ (90¢ buys one U.S. dollar). Economic conditions depress the free trading value to 45¢. For the foreign governments to be competitive with the free market value, the currency will be devalued to 45¢ ($1.80 buys one U.S. dollar).

Note: Devaluation is not a bank's day-to-day fluctuation in exchange rates.

Difference Account

A general ledger account reflecting the cash flow received and paid in settlement monies. The net balance reflects total value debited and credited.

Difference accounts are considered control accounts.

Examples: These accounts include exchange difference account, clearing account, clearing difference account, contract difference account, clearing house account, C/D account.

Differentials

The price difference between classes, grades, and locations for a given commodity. The differential may be a premium paid for better than the contract standard or a discount for lower than contract standard. Differentials are fixed either by the exchange contract terms or as a result of commercial differentials (cotton).

Example: No. 2 Hard Red Winter Wheat meets contract specifications for delivery against the Chicago Board of Trade wheat contract. No. 1 Hard Red Winter Wheat is premium. No. 3 will receive a discount. The grade number reflects quality differential to the flour mill.

Also, wheat awaiting delivery in the Chicago area for the Chicago Board may be more costly than the same wheat being elevated in an Ohio switching district. The differential comes from freight costs to the final destination.

Dirty Float

A currency float or exchange rate that does not float freely, as determined by the market place, but is fixed by government on the basis of national policy.

Disbursement

An immediate payment of money (cash or check).

Disclosed (Omnibus) Account

An omnibus account in which the holder(s) know all of the participating parties.

See: *Undisclosed (Omnibus) Account*

Discount

A downward price adjustment permitted for delivery of a commodity of a lower grade than that specified in the contract.

Example: Delivery of U.S. No. 3 Yellow Soybeans with a given percentage less moisture than standard is discounted against the contract price.

The price difference between futures of different delivery months.

Example:

COMEX Gold June	400.00
COMEX Gold Aug	407.00

June COMEX gold is at a discount under August.

The amount by which the price of one futures contract is below another or below the cash market price.

Example:

	March Wheat
Chicago Board of Trade	363½
Kansas City Board of Trade	372¾
Minneapolis Grain Exchange	394¼

Chicago and Kansas City sell at a discount to Minneapolis.

An amount below par value at which a financial instrument may sell.

Example: Buy at 10% discount

Par Value	$1,000.00
Discount	100.00
Amount Paid	$ 900.00

Discretionary Account

See: *Controlled Account*

Disregard Tape Order

An order given with the customer's agreement that the broker has total discretion over price and time, as well as whether or not to execute all or part of the order.

This term is also known by the standard abbreviation *DRT* or as a *Not Held Order*.

Example:

Buy 5 Apr COMEX Gold 400.00 Not Held

If the broker believes the market is about to go lower, the order can be held without the broker's incurring liability if the market does not, in fact, go lower.

Dock Receipt

An export document that acts as a receipt for goods delivered to a carrier by a shipper.

Documentary Draft

A draft accompanied by a shipping document, such as a bill of lading.

See: *Clean Draft*

Dollar Exchange

Bills of exchange and/or banker's acceptances drawn and/or payable outside the U.S. but payable in U.S. dollars.

Double Bottom

A reversal chart price pattern formed with two sharp price breaks or points indicating the low points reached. The formation creates a "W." See Illustration D-3.

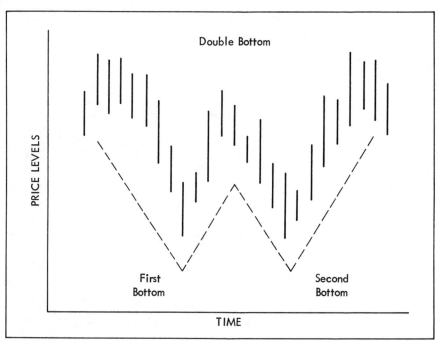

Illustration D-3

Also known as: *"W" Formation*

See: *Double Top*

Double Hedging

The simultaneous hedging of a cash market position by both a futures and an option position. Although a customer is permitted to hold such positions, only one qualifies as a hedge by the exchange.

> **Example:** On March 1 a silver dealer agrees to deliver 5,000 ounces of silver three months hence at a price of $7.30 per ounce.

To protect this price, the silver dealer purchases a May silver futures contract at 72500, thereby assuring the dealer of paying or replacing the metal for less than what the metal was sold.

To minimize the futures exposure on the downside and provide a repricing ability, the dealer purchases a May silver put, strike price 730, at 34.00.

If at time of delivery, the cash price is

Higher	Deliver cash metal	7.3000 cr
	Sell the long May futures	
	Bgt 7.2500	
	Sold 7.950	.7000 cr
	Abandon Put option (cost)	.3400 dr
	Net price received	7.6600 cr
	Cost of metal (futures purchase)	7.2500 dr
	Net profit	.4100 cr
Lower	Deliver cash metal	$7.3000 cr
	Exercise May put 730	
	Bgt 72.500	
	Short 73.000 (exer)	.0500 cr
	Less cost of option	.3400 dr
	Net price received	7.0100 cr
	Cost of metal (current cash price)	6.6000 Cr
	Net profit	.4100 cr

Note: Either the cash may be hedged with the futures or the option may be spread with the futures.

Double Option

A London nontraded option that gives the buyer the right to enter into a contract as seller or buyer at a given strike price.

Example:

Double Option Granted	
Quantity	10 lots Sugar #4 (50 tonnes/lot)
Delivery	December Whole or Part
Strike	£ 115.50/tonne
Premium	£ 20 per tonne
Declaration	November 20 (noon)

A double premium is paid for the privilege of the double option:

Premium	2 (10 lots × 50 tonnes @ 20)
Premium	20,000 pounds sterling

If by November 20 the market advances, the taker declares the option a call and receives the sugar.

If by November 20 the market declines, the taker declares the option a put and sells the sugar.

Double Top

A reversal chart price pattern formed with two sharp peaks indicating maximum levels reached. The formation creates an "M." See Illustration D-4.

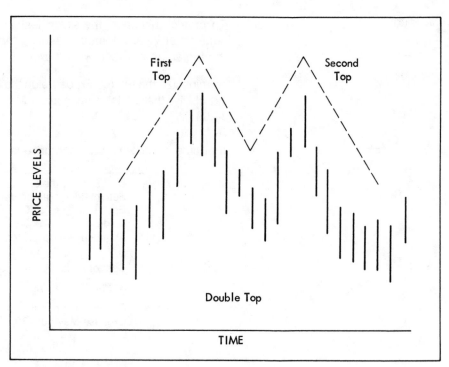

Illustration D-4

Also known as: *"M" Formation*

See: *Double Bottom*

Down Trend

A price pattern established by new, lower low prices and new, lower high prices. The upper limits form a straight downward line on a bar chart. See Illustration D-5.

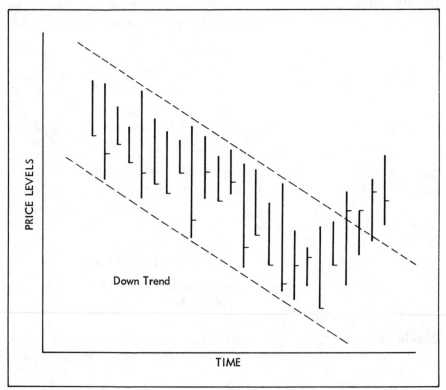

Illustration D-5

Also known as: *Trending Down*

See: *Trending Up/Up Trend*

Down Tick

A price lower than the immediately preceding sale price.

Also known as: *Minus Tick*

Example:
New York Futures Exchange—Composit Index

Trading:	9:00 a.m.	Trade 1	88.00
	9:03 a.m.	Trade 2	88.00
	9:10 a.m.	Trade 3	88.05
	9:15 a.m.	Trade 4	88.00

Trade 4 represents a *down tick*.

See: *Plus Tick*
Zero Minus Tick

Draft

See: *Bill of Exchange*

Drawee

An individual or company upon which demand for payment of a draft is made.

See: *Drawer*
Payee

Drawer

An individual or company issuing and/or executing a draft for payment.

See: *Drawee*
Payee

DRT

See: *Disregard Tape*

Dual Option

A granted call option is matched, for margin purposes, with a granted put involving the same underlying commodity.

This term is sometimes called a *straddle*. (The call converts to a short future and the put to a long futures.)

Example:
Short 1 Mar 8X Composit Index Call 85.00
Short 1 June 8X Composit Index Put 87.00

See: *Option/Option Spreads*

Dual Trading

The practice of acting as an agent, buying and selling for the accounts of others, while also trading one's own account.

In futures and options trading, the agent may not trade against orders solicited or received without explicit permission from the client. If the agent trades his/her own orders along with the customers' orders, the customers' orders must be filled first.

Dutiable goods

Any goods requiring, by law, import or export duties.

Duty

A government tax on imports and/or exports.

Also known as: *Tariff*

Duty Free

Imports free, by law, of any custom duties.

Effective Date

The date an agreement or trade goes into effect as specified by the contract, an order, or some other document.

>**Example:** February 15 a buyer contracts for 15 tonnes of rubber. The contract calls for three equal delivery dates:

	5 tonnes Mar 15
	5 tonnes Apr 15
	5 tonnes May 15
February 15 =	effective date of the contract
March 15 =	effective date first delivery
April 15 =	effective date second delivery
May 15 =	effective date third delivery

EFP

The standard abbreviation for *Exchange for Physicals*.

See: *AA/Against Actuals*

Eligible Margin

Cash or other collateral specified by the exchange as an acceptable means of satisfying margin requirements.

>**Example:**
>U.S. Government obligations (T-Bills)
>Warehouse receipts
>NYSE and AMEX traded stocks and bonds

Note: Eligible margin varies from exchange to exchange.

See: *Margin Requirements*

Embargo

A formal ban on trade placed by a government or private organization.

Emergency

A sudden, unexpected turn of events that prevents the market from reflecting normal supply and demand of a commodity, thus requiring immediate action in order to maintain orderly trading.

Example:
Market emergencies such as excessive volume
Physical emergencies such as weather or computer malfunctions
Political emergencies, such as assassinations or declarations of war
Economic emergencies such as a monetary crisis

Emergency Action

An exchange rule, generally short term, imposed because of a sudden, unexpected turn of events that causes undue influence in the market place by severely restricting its orderly behavior.

Example:
Delay of morning opening
Extending the time for deliveries
Increasing margins
Suspending trading

Endorse

To sign a document and thereby pass title.

Endorsee

One to whom endorsement and delivery is made.

See: *Endorser*

Endorsement

The signature that makes a document negotiable.

See: *Blank Endorsement/Endorsement in Blank*
Conditional Endorsement
Qualified Endorsement
Restrictive Endorsement
Special Endorsement

Endorsement in Blank

See: *Blank Endorsement*

Endorser

The signer of the document that passes title.

See: *Endorsee*

Enter Open Stop

An instruction to enter a stop order after the execution of a previous order has taken place. The instruction may be submitted as a separate order or contingent to a primary order. This term is also known by the standard abbreviation *EOS*.

Example:

EOS Sell 5 May Pork Bellies @ 3400

may also be written as

S 5 K BLY @ 3400 X GTC

The above order was submitted as a separate instruction and is good until cancelled.

Buy 5 May Pork Bellies @ 3600
    when done EOS Sell 5 @ 3400

may also be written as

B 5 K BLY @ 3600
EOS S 5 @ 3400

This instruction consists of two separate orders. The EOS is not entered until after the purchase is made.

Note: EOS instructions are generally placed somewhat away from the current trading level and are used to minimize loss on an existing open position.

EOS

See: *Enter Open Stop*

Equity

Residual value of an account if all open positions were closed at current market value.

Equity = Cash
    + Market value of positions
        (open trade profits
        less open trade losses)

Example:

Cash in Account	$ 1,000	
Securities on Deposit	10,000	
Open Positions		

		Trade Price	Settle Price
Long 1 Oct COMEX Gold	396.40	396.00	
Short 2 Dec COMEX Gold	398.00	400.00	
Loss on Long		40.00	
Profit on Short		400.00	
Net		360.00 (profit)	

Equity = Cash (1,000) + Market Value (360)
Equity = $1,360

Note: Securities on deposit are not included in this value.

Equity Interest

A financial share that empowers the owner to have full or limited control of a given entity in proportion to the equity invested.

Eurocurrency

Deposits made and held outside the borders of the originating country.

    Example: Eurodollars are U.S. dollars held abroad.

Evening Up

Generally, the method by which a floor broker zeros out his/her own account or that of a client to reduce exposure. The whole position, rather than a specific trade(s), is offset or straddled.

This term is also used loosely to mean *offset* or *closeout.*

    Example: A floor broker is long 100 lots of a given commodity and does not want to assume the risk of holding the position overnight. The broker sells 100 lots and has no position at the closing bell.

    Also, a floor broker is long 100 December lots of a given commodity, but December is not liquid enough to sell 100 lots. The broker sells 100 March of the given commodity and creates a straddle position.

    These actions reduce the exposure risks but do not eliminate them completely.

Note: If the trader is unable to execute either of the transactions in the examples, he/she may go to a related market for protection.

Even Lot

A full contract or quantity of a commodity equal in size to the futures contract of that commodity.

Also known as: *Round Lot*

Example:

	Cash		Futures
	5,000 bushels grain	=	1 grain contract
	37,500 lbs. coffee	=	1 coffee contract
	4,950 bushels grain	=	no equivalent
	38,000 lbs. coffee	=	no equivalent

See: *Job Lot/Odd Lot*

Excess

A value over total requirements, not including securities on deposit, for a given day.

Excess = equity less requirements

Example:

Cash in Account	$1,000
Net Market Value of Positions	360
Equity	1,360
Margin Requirement	750

Excess = equity (1,360) − requirements (750)
Excess = $610

See: *Deficit*

Exchange Against Actuals

See: *AA/Against Actuals/Exchange for/of, or for/Cash Commodity for Futures*

Exchange (Domestic)

A financial institution authorized by the Commodity Futures Trading Commission to be responsible for the governing rules and regulations and providing an open, fair market place to trade commodity contracts.

Exchange-Certified Stocks

Stocks of commodities held in depositories and certified by the governing exchange authority as constituting available "good delivery" against a given futures contract.

Exchange Committee

A group of two or more exchange members that conducts investigations, advises and assists the exchange board, and performs any specified duties necessary to carry out the rules, regulations, and objectives of the exchange.

Exchange Controls

A government's restrictions on the free international exchange of foreign currencies within its own boundaries.

Exchange Fee

The small sum charged per contract by an exchange for providing facilities for executing a trade transaction; or the sum charged for a service offered by the exchange.

Example:

Fee per contract	$ .50
Fee for floor clerk badge	$20.00

Exchange Fine

A sum levied by an exchange for violation of exchange rules.

Exchange Floor

The area of an exchange, commonly consisting of rings or pits, in which trading by open outcry takes place. See Illustration E-1.

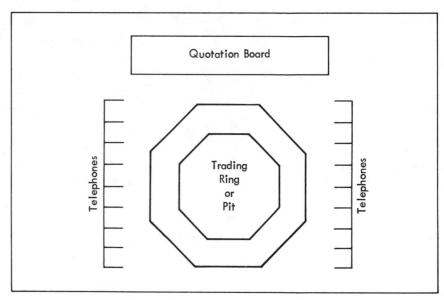

Illustration E-1

Also known as: *Trading Floor*

Exchange for/of . . .	The beginning of various phrases that express an exchange between actuals and futures.
	See: *AA/Against Actuals/Cash Commodity for Futures*
Exchange Member	An individual and/or stockholder who purchases a membership in a given authorized exchange and has the voting rights and privileges of that exchange.
Exchange Minimum	The least amount of initial margin required by an exchange in order to hold a given commodity contract.
	Severe penalties are incurred by any member who permits a lower rate.
Exchange Rate	The price of one country's currency in terms of another.

Example:

British pounds to U.S. dollars
1.4525 pound sterling = $1.00

Note: Rates fluctuate constantly.

Exchange Reporter	An employee of a given exchange responsible for reporting for public notice market prices as they occur. This individual is stationed in or immediately adjacent to the trading area.
Executing Broker	A member of an exchange who executes orders for an account or himself/herself in the trading ring or pit of that exchange.

Also known as: *Floor Broker or Pit Broker*

Note: *Floor broker* and *pit broker* are terms actually used to describe the profession; *executing broker* signifies a broker's function in a transaction.

See: *Broker*
Carrying Broker
Floor Trader/Market Maker
Trader
Two-Dollar Broker

Exercise

The conversion of a long option contract to the underlying futures contract at the specified, contracted strike price. A call is exercised into a long futures, a put into a short futures. Exercise is elective by the holder of a long position.

Example: Consider COMEX Gold, with option expires on the second Friday prior to futures expiration:

December COMEX Gold: November 9 (expiration)

Position as of September 10:

Customer A Long COMEX Gold Call @ 400.00
Customer B Long COMEX Gold Put @ 440.00
Customer C Long COMEX Gold Call @ 380.00

On September 10 exercise "A" and the call becomes

Long 1 Dec COMEX Gold @ 400.00 (futures)

On September 27 exercise "B" and the put becomes

Short 1 Dec COMEX Gold @ 440.00 (futures)

On November 9 exercise "C" and the call becomes

Long 1 Dec COMEX Gold 380.00 (futures)

Note: Some exchanges may automatically exercise an in-the-money option on the expiration date.

This term is also used in the conversion of an option to the underlying actual commodity.

See: *Assignment*

Exercise Date

The day the option is converted to a futures or actuals.

Example: Using the situation in the example *Exercise*:

Customer A *Exercise Date*	Sept 10
Customer B	Sept 27
Customer C	Nov 9

Exercise Price

The predetermined price level(s) at which an underlying futures contract or actual commodity may be established upon exercise of the option.

For futures options, the exchange sets a price, in line with the previous day's settlement price for the underlying futures. From that price, exercise prices at exchange-determined intervals above and below are established. Options may be traded at these exercise prices. Each successive day, new prices may be established in addition to those currently trading and/or available for trading if the futures market fluctuations warrant it.

Also known as: *Strike Price or Striking Price*

Example:

Settlement Price of May 20	Eligible Exercise Prices for May 21	
Futures	Call	Put
	440.00	440.00
	420.00	420.00
December 399.50	400.00*	400.00*
	380.00	380.00
	360.00	360.00

*The central point, at-the-money, is the one closest to the equivalent 399.50.

Note: Price increments vary from commodity to commodity.

Exhaustion Gap

On a chart, a significant breakaway following a lengthy sharp movement in a given direction that may indicate a key reversal. See Illustration E-2.

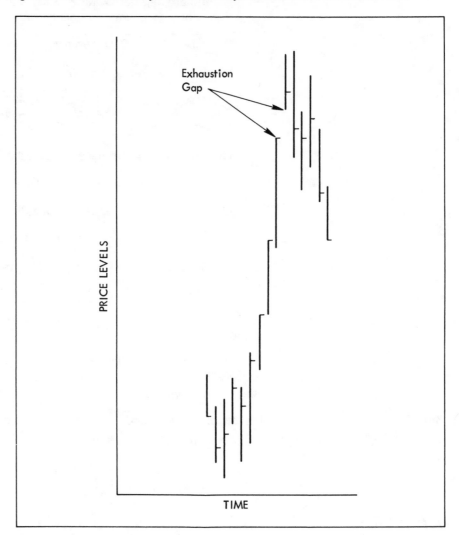

Illustration E-2

See: *Breakaway Gap*
Common Gap
Gap
Runaway Gap

Expanded Limits

Points added to a standard contract limit to provide depth to the market. Governed by exchange rules, this practice adds liquidity to the market when normal market contract limits no longer stabilize activity.

Note: Most exchange rules require the market to have achieved two to three limit move days immediately preceding the day the expanded-limit rule is incorporated.

Example: COMEX Gold's normal price limit is $25. Trading in June for August COMEX Gold may look like this:

	Permitted Daily Range	Settlement Price
June 11	350.00 – 400.00	400.00 limit up
June 12	375.00 – 425.00	425.00 limit up
June 13	400.00 – 450.00	450.00 limit up

Limit-up moves of 2,500 points each of the above days. For the purposes of the example, this activates the expanded-limit rule: 50% increase, to the contract standard 2,500 points.

June 14	412.50–487.50 range 50% greater (425.00–475.00 comparison)

For exact specifications regarding expanded limits for an individual commodity, refer to the exchange offering that contract.

Expiration

See: *Abandonment*

Expiration Date

The last day that an option may be exercised into the underlying futures/actual commodity contract; if not exercised or assigned, the option ceases to exist. See Illustration E-3.

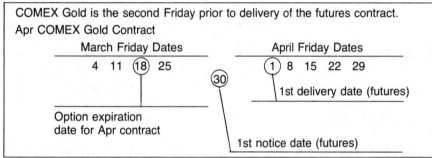

COMEX Gold is the second Friday prior to delivery of the futures contract.
Apr COMEX Gold Contract

Illustration E-3

Note: An exchange may rule automatic exercise for in-the-money options.

Also known as: *Declaration Date (for London options)*

Note: Declaration date is agreed to between buyer and seller for nontraded options and exchange-determined for traded options.

Ex-pit

A (legal) trade made outside the ring or pit of the exchange and primarily used in price-fixing transactions involving the purchase of actual commodities at a specified basis.

In an ex-pit trade the basis is established, the futures transaction is made determining actual dollars and cents for the cash commodity, and the floor brokers complete the transaction outside the ring. An ex-pit must involve settlement of a cash transaction.

> **Example:** The holder of cash gold bullion is willing to sell the bullion to a smelter but wishes to maintain a long gold position at the same time. An agreement is made to sell the bullion for a determined cash price and receive an equivalent number of futures contracts priced 20 cents under April COMEX gold. The transactions are as follows:
>
> The holder of the bullion sells 1,000 ounces of gold to the smelter for $400 per ounce. Cash market is $380.

The smelter sells to the bullion holder 10 Apr COMEX gold contracts (ex-pit) at 400. Futures market is trading at 420.

The smelter now owns the metal. The bullion seller is long 10 April COMEX gold contracts equivalent to 1000 ounces of bullion. The transaction is reflected as ex-pit on official transaction records.

Note: The 10 futures contract sold by the smelter may offset existing long positions being held or the smelter may have to buy back the sale at his/her own risk in the auction market.

The movement of a futures or option position from one clearing member to another or to another account of the same ownership by election of the client, the clearing member, or the clearing house. The agreement is made outside the trading ring and all parties must be in agreement. There is no change of ownership of the trade. The original price and date of the trade must be affixed and maintained.

Also known as: *Transfer Trade, Office Trade*

Export

Goods originating in one country that are sold and shipped to another country.

To send (ship) these goods abroad.

See: *Import(s)*

Export Dec

The standard abbreviation for *export declaration*, a source document for export statistics required by the U.S. Department of Commerce to control exports. All particulars about a shipment are located on this document.

Export Declaration

See: *Export Dec*

Export Document

A written instrument that furnishes information or serves as evidence, proof, or support of exported goods: for example, export declaration, dock receipt, etc.

See: *Import Document*

Export License

A government-issued document authorizing the exportation of goods.

See: *Import License*

Export Quota

A limitation placed by a government on the types and quantities of goods eligible for exportation.

See: *Import Quota*

Face Value

The amount stamped or printed on an instrument of value, such as coins or currency. This amount indicates the stated value when issued or at maturity.

Also known as: *Par Value*

> **Example:** A stock certificate may have a face value of $1.00. The market value may, however, be many times $1.00, for it reflects the firm's capital assets and expected earnings.
>
> U.S. Treasury bills are offered in a minimum face value amount of $10,000. The bill trades at a discount, the interest to be earned on its face value up to the time of maturity.

See: *Market Value*

Factor

The constant value of a minimum price fluctuation for a given commodity, which, when multiplied by the futures price and quantity, results in the value of a contract.

> **Example:**
>
> | Commodity | Minimum Fluctuation | Factor |
> |---|---|---|
> | Sugar | .01 | 11.20 |
> | Wheat | ¼ | 12.50 |
> | Swiss francs | .00010 | 1.25 |
> | Gold | .10 | 10.00 |

An entity that purchases accounts receivable at a discount and assumes risks and collection responsibility in exchange for profits made on the discounted rate.

A consignment agent working for commission on goods sold, remitting sales revenue to the owners of the goods.

Factor Decimal (Indicator)	The way a commodity (factor) is expressed or the pricing units a commodity is traded in.

> **Example:**
> .01 cents
> .02-½ cents
> .10 cents
> .0001 cents
> 1/64th of a dollar
> ¼ cents

Fannie Mae	An abbreviated form of Federal National Mortgage Association and the name of its instruments. The Association, also abbreviated FNMA, is a federally sponsored private corporation that deals in government-insured and/or guaranteed mortgages.
Farm Cooperative	A joint form of business organized by farmers for such economic purposes as buying equipment and supplies and marketing produce. Members are stock- or shareholders.
Farmer's Credit Administration	A federal agency responsible for the administration of credit alternatives for farmers. There are 12 farm credit districts in the United States. Each district has a Federal Land Bank, a Federal Intermediate Credit Bank, and a Bank for Cooperatives. Appointed by the President of the United States, members from each district comprise the Federal Farm Credit Board, which sets the Farmer's Credit Administration's policies.
	Also known as: *FCA*
Farmer's Home Association	An agency of the Department of Agriculture that makes affordable loans to farmers for a variety of purposes, such as homes, land, operating expenses, etc.
Farm Surplus	Farm produce being held or destroyed, generally in accordance with government policy and support payments. Farm surplus is considered unsalable at current market prices in the available market place.
FAS	The standard abbreviation for *Free Alongside Ship*. FAS is an export price quote that includes all costs up to the point the goods are directly available for loading on the ship.
Fast Market	A condition arising from strong interest by buyers and/or sellers causing the market to move rapidly and broadly. Price levels may be skipped and bid and offer quotations occur so rapidly that they cannot be fully reported.

> **Example:** a review of a 30-second tape shows
> _____
> *Normal market*
> 3.24, 3.24¼, 3.24, 24 . . . .
>
> *Fast market*
> 3.24, ¼, ½, 24, ½, ¾, ¼, ½, 3.25, 24½, 25 . . .
> _____

FCA	**See:** *Farmer's Credit Administration*
FCIC	The standard abbreviation for the *Federal Crop Insurance Corporation*, an agency of the Department of Agriculture responsible for a national system of federally funded insurance against natural and unavoidable crop loss, due to such occurrences as weather or insects.

| **FCM** | The standard abbreviation for *futures commission merchant*, an individual, association, partnership, or corporation registered by the Commodity Futures Trading Commission to solicit and/or accept orders for the purchase or sale of futures and option contracts, as well as money deposits or other collateral to secure the contracts. The FCM receives compensation for these services. |

Federal Crop Insurance Corp.

See: *FCIC*

Federal Funds

Funds held by Federal Reserve member banks in excess of legal requirements. A bank's federal funds are available for loan to under-reserve-fund member banks at less than the federal discount rate.

Federal Funds Rate

The discount rate fixed by the Federal Reserve Board. It represents the rate banks must pay when borrowing money from the Federal Reserve Banks. This rate influences credit conditions.

> **Example:** If the Federal Rate increases, private interest rates increase; if the Federal Rate decreases, private interest rates decrease.

Federal Intermediate Credit Banks

Twelve banks that, as part of the farm credit system of the Farmer's Credit Administration, provide reserves for and lend to production credit associations, which in turn lend to farmers.

Federal Land Banks

Twelve banks that, as part of the farm credit system of the Farmer's Credit Administration, provide long-term (5–10 year) mortgage loans at favorable rates to members of land-bank associations.

Federal National Mortgage Association

See: *Fannie Mae*

Federal Reserve System

The U.S. federal banking system, which consists of 12 federal reserve districts and a board of governors empowered to influence and centralize the direction of U.S. monetary and credit policy.

Note: The federal reserve districts consist of about 5,700 bank members. All national banks must join; state banks may join if they meet specified requirements.

The Board of Governors of the Federal Reserve System is appointed by the President of the United States.

Federal Register

A central publication of federal proclamations, orders, regulations, notices, and other legal documents.

Fee

A sum charged for a service or privilege.

See: *Clearing Fee*
      Exchange Fee
      Member Fee

Feeder

An overland transportation line connected with one or more lines accessing a larger area.

An animal being fattened for slaughter, feeder cattle, a commodity product.

FIFO

The standard abbreviation for *first in, first out*, a method of selection and matching in offsetting positions in which a given buy or sell transaction will offset the earliest trade date of the given commodity month sell or buy on file for the given customer.

Example:

Open position for account ABC on the morning of March 11:

Long	Mar 1	2 Dec Gold @ 402.00
	Mar 3	2 Dec Gold @ 400.00
	Mar 10	3 Dec Gold @ 404.00
	Mar 10	1 Dec Gold @ 402.00

On March 11, account ABC enters a sell order:

Sell 1 Dec COMEX Gold @ 402.00

The sell would select one of the March 1 positions and liquidate or offset it, leaving one March 1 position remaining.

Note: Quantity and price are not taken into consideration for a match.

At the close of March 11, the account open position is:

Long	Mar 1	1 Dec Gold @ 402.00
	Mar 3	2 Dec Gold @ 400.00
	Mar 10	3 Dec Gold @ 404.00
	Mar 10	1 Dec Gold @ 402.00

On March 12, account ABC enters a sell order:

Sell 3 Dec COMEX Gold @ 403.00

FIFO application would offset (liquidate) one March 1 long position at 402.00 and two March 3 long positions at 400.00.

At the close of March 12, the account open position is:

Long	Mar 10	3 Dec Gold @ 404.00
	Mar 10	1 Dec Gold @ 402.00

Note: FIFO is the method generally used to offset positions in a commodity futures trading account.

Sometimes used to describe an account that uses this method of trade selection (as opposed to the *instruct* method).

Example: In the above example, account ABC is a FIFO account.

The trade transaction using this method of selection and ultimate liquidation.

The buy and sell offset is called a FIFO liquidation.

See: *Instruct*
LIFO

A method of inventory selection and evaluation in which the earliest items purchased are the earliest items used for distribution or evaluation.
See: *LIFO*

Fill or Kill

An order that must be offered or bid immediately at a given price and cancelled if not executed. The standard abbreviation is *FOK*.

Also known as: *Immediate Order, FOK*

Example:

Buy 1 Dec COMEX Gold @ 400.00 Fill or Kill

may also be written as

B 1 Z COMEX GLD @ 400.00 FOK

Finance Bill	A bill of exchange drawn on a bank in one country by a bank in another country and, generally, based on good faith and credit of the drawer. A finance bill may function as an advance of funds.
Financial Futures	Contracts for future delivery of a specified amount of government or private indebtedness. The market value or discount value is determined at the time of the contract between buyer and seller on the given exchange.

Also known as: *Financial Instrument Futures*

> **Example:**
> Treasury bond
> Treasury bill
> Treasury note
> Commercial paper
> Ginnie Mae

Fineness	The degree or proportion of purity after refining a precious metal.

A fineness of 99.9 is the closest to absolute purity that can be obtained.

> **Example:** A 100-ounce gold bar may be 99.9 fineness.

> In order to use this purity efficiently in coinage or jewelry, an alloy is added and measured in karats.

> An 18K gold ring is 18 parts gold and 6 parts alloy.

FIP	The standard abbreviation for *Free in Pipeline*, a term of delivery in a contract or an option given a buyer of a crude oil contract.
Firm Number	An alphabetical or, more often, numerical identifier assigned by a clearing house to each clearing member.

An account identifier assigned by a firm to its customers and vendors.

First In, First Out	**See:** *FIFO*
First Notice Day	The first day on which the seller (holder of a short position) may issue notice of the intention to deliver the actual commodity against the futures market position to the holder of the long position. First notice day varies by commodity and exchange. In some commodity markets, cash settlement may occur in lieu of delivery of the commodity.

Also known as: *Notice Day*

> **Example:** The first notice day for a commodity is two business days prior to the first calendar business day of April.

> Notice days are March 30 through April 27 if all days are business days.

Note: The two-day lag for delivery is the time required to prepare for receiving the delivery. The buyer in the futures does not control what date in the delivery month delivery may be made.

Fishybacking	A method of freight transportation in which two types of vehicles are used at once, one of which is a water carrier.

> **Example:** A truck loaded with goods is itself loaded onto a barge.

See: *Piggybacking*

Fixing the Price

Agreement between buyer and seller to determine the price at which a cash commodity will be invoiced. This price is based on a specified number of points on or off a specified futures. This agreement is generally made with actuals but may also be used in futures against actuals. When futures are involved, the agreement takes place outside the ring or pit.

A buy-and-sell basis is established; fixed prices on the purchase and sales are determined later.

> **Example:** Using the Cash Market: An elevator operator owns wheat at $3.00 per bushel and is hedged at $3.05 per bushel. A miller wishes to buy wheat in the near future. The miller enters into an agreement with the operator to buy the wheat at 1¢ off the futures price over the next 60 days. The elevator operator agrees.
>
> Twenty days later, the nearby futures price is trading at $2.50 per bushel. The miller calls for the wheat at $2.49 per bushel.

Note: The fixing at $2.49 can only occur when the futures market reaches the level of $2.50.

Prices are not established until an agreed event occurs to determine the invoice price. Futures may or may not be involved at some point.

> **Example:** Using Futures Market: The elevator operator owns wheat at $3.00 per bushel and is hedged at $3.05 per bushel. The miller wishes to buy wheat in the near future and asks to purchase a buyer's call to buy the wheat at 1¢ off the December futures during the next 60 days. The elevator operator agrees.
>
> Twenty days later, the December futures wheat contract is selling at $2.50 per bushel. The miller calls the floor and purchases a December wheat futures contract at $2.50 and gives it up to the elevator operator's account.
>
> The elevator operator and miller confirm the transaction. The miller now is invoiced at $2.49 per bushel for the cash sale.

Note: The fixing at $2.49 is based on the agreement of 1¢ off December futures. It cannot be established until the futures is purchased.

Flag

A chart price pattern in which the lines connecting the highs and lows move parallel in a fixed range. The flag pattern interrupts the trend. See Illustration F-1.

Flexible Exchange Rate

A system in which the currency exchange rate varies freely against other currencies according to supply and demand.

Flexible Tariff

A tariff that can be adjusted, generally within specified bounds and/or on a contingency basis.

Floating Exchange Rate

A system in which the value of a currency fluctuates freely against other currencies according to supply and demand versus a fixed rate established and controlled by governments.

Also known as: *Fluctuating Exchange Rate*

Floating Policy

An insurance contract that remains in force until cancelled. Premium is paid as shipment is made and cargo afloat and in transit is covered as described in the contract.

Also known as: *Open Policy*

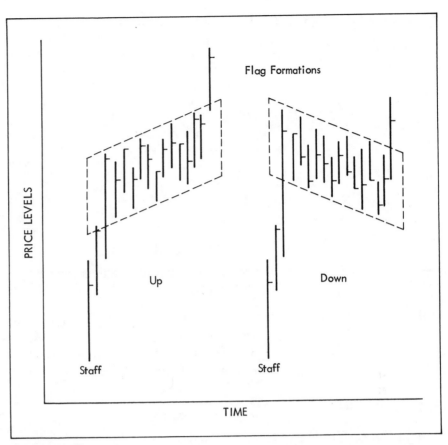

Illustration F-1

See: *Blanket Policy*
Special Risk Policy

Floor

The location provided by the exchange for members to meet and execute orders.

Floor Broker

An individual who executes orders in the pit for himself/herself, others, or a futures commission merchant.

Also known as: *Pit Trader*

See: *Broker*
Carrying Broker
Floor Trader/Market Maker
Trader
Two-Dollar Broker

Floor Trader

An individual who trades for his/her own account on the floor of the exchange.

Also known as: *Market Maker*

See: *Broker*
Executing Broker/Floor Broker/Pit Trader
Trader

Floor Transaction

The individual trade agreement between a buyer and seller carried out in the trading ring or pit of an exchange by members of that exchange.

Fluctuating Exchange Rate **See:** *Floating Exchange Rate*

Fluctuation The movement of prices as stated in gradations such as points or fractions of points or cents or dollars and cents.

Fluctuations are caused by the willingness of buyers and sellers to give and take on price value.

> **Example:** Consider April COMEX Gold:

Trade		
1	461.40	
2	461.50	up 10
3	461.40	down 10
4	461.30	down 10
5	461.50	up 20
6	461.60	up 10

Note: Each change in price from the previous price cannot be less than a minimum fluctuation. These movements are not restricted by time, such as minutes, hours, or days.

FOB The standard abbreviation for *Free on Board*. An indication that the costs of putting the commodity on the carrier—delivery, inspections, and boarding costs—have all been paid for by the seller. Costs of transporting to point of destination are not included and are the responsibility of the buyer, as are all other risks.

FOK **See:** *Fill or Kill*

Foreign Bill (of Exchange) A bill of exchange drawn on a drawee in one country and payable in another country.

Also known as: *Foreign Draft, Foreign Exchange*

Foreign Currency Currency or medium of exchange, circulation, and record-keeping of any foreign country.

Foreign Draft **See:** *Foreign Bill (of Exchange)*

Foreign Exchange The means by which international financial transactions are handled or traded (with denominations in several currencies, including U.S. dollars).

The equivalent or financial instrument itself.

See: *Foreign Bill (of Exchange)*

Foreign Exchange Market The worldwide market for currencies of those countries in which settling of international obligations and trading in world currencies and currency futures takes place. The foreign exchange market is in various locations throughout the world rather than in one central place. National and international banks make up this market.

Foreign Exchange Rate The relative purchasing power of different nations' currencies.

The rate at which a unit of one currency is exchanged for a unit of another currency.

> **Example:** $1.50 in U.S. dollars buys 1 British pound sterling. Three Swiss francs buys 2½ Deutsche marks.

Foreign Exchange Reserves The amount of foreign currency and/or financial instruments held by a government in its monetary reserves.

Foreign Trade	Trade between public and/or private parties in one country with those of another country. Foreign trade consists of importing and exporting.
Forfeiture	The loss of money or rights due to failure to fulfill obligations.
Forward Contract	An agreement to buy and sell a cash commodity for delivery some time in the future.
	Terms of the contract are agreed to immediately. These contracts are usually for short terms, such as 30, 60, or 90 days.
	Unlike the futures contract, a forward contract is generally not standardized and is not transferable.
	See: *Futures Contract*
Forward Exchange	Foreign exchange bought and sold at current prices for future delivery. Forward exchange has all characteristics of the forward market; however, delivery and settlement are generally two days from the agreement.
Forwarding Agent	A freighting firm that consolidates a number of small shipments into one, handling papers and obtaining price advantages for the larger shipment. Used primarily in exporting.
	Also known as: *Freight Forwarder*
Forward Market	A medium for actual commodities to be traded for some delivery other than immediate. This market is not centralized and exists primarily on individual agreement. Contracts in this market need not be standard.
	See: *Cash Market/Spot Market* *Futures Market*
Forward Movement	An upward trend of market prices measured for a specified time, such as hour(s), month(s), or year(s).
Free Alongside Ship	**See:** *FAS*
Free in Pipeline	**See:** *FIP*
Free on Board	**See:** *FOB*
Free Supply	The physical amount of a given commodity available for trading at a given time. Free supply is world stock less government holdings.
	Note: This term is not to be confused with *deliverable supply*.
Free Trade	A system of international trade without government-imposed restrictions, such as tariffs.
Free Trade Area	Two or more countries that agree upon free trade between them but set trade restrictions with other countries.
Free Trade Zone	An area (or port) with no import or export duties on goods.
Freight	Goods transported by land, air, or sea.
	Charges for transporting goods.
Freight Absorption	The payment of freight by the seller of the goods.

Freight Bill Receipt

An import document evidencing that freight charges for cargo have been paid. It is presented at the pier to obtain release of the cargo.

Also known as: *Freight Release*

Freighter

A ship primarily carrying freight.

Freight Forwarder

See: *Forwarding Agent*

Freight Line

A transporting company primarily carrying freight.

Freight Release

See: *Freight Bill Receipt*

Fundamental Analysis

A type of market analysis that stresses supply and demand as the basis for determining trends and prices.

See: *Cyclic Analysis*
Historical Analysis
Technical Analysis

Futures Contract

An agreement to buy (receive) or sell (deliver) a standard amount of a commodity for a specified month in the future under the terms and conditions established by an organized exchange on which trading is conducted via open outcry to determine the price and trades cleared via the clearing house.

See: *Forward Contract*

Futures Market

A market where traders buy and sell futures and/or option contracts to receive or deliver a specified quantity and grade of a commodity at a specified future time. The contracts are offered by authorized Boards of Trade commonly known as commodity exchanges.

Note: The futures market consists of contracts in commodities, foreign exchange, and government obligations.

FX

See: *Foreign Exchange*

Gap

On a price chart, a blank space representing a price(s) at which the commodity did not trade. See Illustration G-1.

See: *Breakaway Gap*
Common Gap
Exhaustion Gap
Runaway Gap

General Ledger

The primary accounting ledger of an entity. This document contains detailed and/or summary information on all business accounting activity.

Ginnie Mae

An abbreviation of *Government National Mortgage Association* and the name for instruments of that association. Ginnie Mae (also abbreviated GNMA) is a federally owned and financed corporation that deals in high-risk mortgages.

Give up

The action of a floor broker or brokerage firm giving an executed order to a third party for booking.

Example: Customer A gives an order to broker B and instructs broker B to give the execution to broker C for the account of customer A.

Glut

A market condition in which supply far exceeds demand (consumption and price). This term is primarily used for agricultural products.

Gold Reserve

The amount of gold being physically held by a government as a support to currency and/or obligations.

Gold Exchange Standard

The system in which a currency is officially convertible into gold at a guaranteed, fixed price.

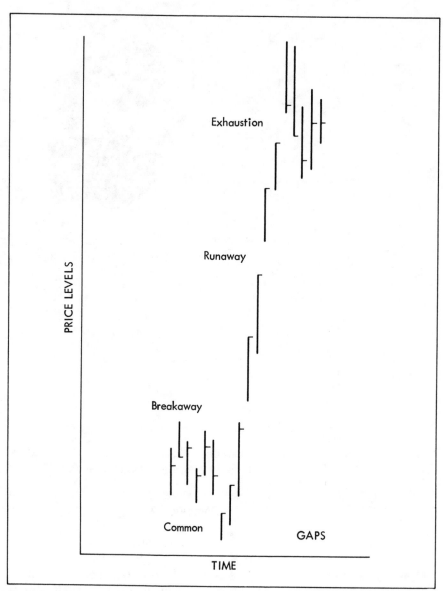

Illustration G-1

Gold Standard

A system based on gold or gold coins in which a currency's domestic and international value is kept stable in terms of a fixed gold price.

Good Til Cancelled

An order to buy or sell at a fixed price that remains open until executed or cancelled by the customer.

Example:

Buy 1 Dec COMEX Gold @ 420.00 Good-Til-Cancelled

may also be written as

B 1 Z COMEX GLD @ 420.00 GTC

Note: Provision may be made to cancel automatically on a given day.

Example: An order entered on March 10

Buy 1 Dec COMEX Gold @ 420.00 Good-Til Mar 15

may also be written as

Also known as: *Open Order or Resting Order or by the standard abbreviation GTC*

Government Bill

A short-term government debt obligation.

Government Bond

A government (or agency of the government) issued debt obligation in the form of a bond.

Government National Mortgage Association

See: *Ginnie Mae*

GPM

The standard abbreviation for *Gross Processing Margin*. A formula used to express the relationship between raw material costs to sales income from finished products.

> **Example:** With soybeans, it is the difference between the cost of soybeans and the combined sales income from the oil and meal resulting from the processing of those beans.

Grades

Various qualities of a given commodity used to establish standards acceptable in trade usage.

See: *Basis Grade*

Grading

The classification, identification, and application of a set of quality standards for a given commodity.

Grading Certificate

A certificate attesting to the quality of a given quantity of a commodity as determined by an official inspector, tester, or grader.

Grain on Consignment

A standard contract term for grain transferred to a broker for the purpose of sale in the cash market.

Grantor

The seller of a futures, cash, or options contract. The grantor is said to hold a short position.

Note: This term is most commonly used in writing options.

Also known as: *Seller or Writer*

Gross

Total before deductions but after all corrections and adjustments.

See: *Net*

Gross Margining

A procedure of applying margin requirements to all account positions of record. Gross margining maintains financial integrity of the account.

> **Example:** Broker ABC is a clearing member of clearing association A, which requires gross margining. The broker also clears with clearing association B, which permits net margins. Both associations require $1000.00 per contract. See Illustration G-2.

Notes:
Clearing house margins are separate from exchange requirements.

Gross margining is required, by regulation, on domestic omnibus accounts in which the account shows a long and short open position in the same contract month of a commodity. This regulation is not binding for foreign omnibus accounts.

Book Position of ABC Company (all customers)

Association A (Gross Margining)	Commodity May Light Crude Oil		
	Long	100	contracts
	Short	50	contracts
		150	gross
Requirement	(times)	$ 1,000	per contract
		$150,000	deposit

Versus

Association B (Net Margining)	Commodity May Unleaded Gasoline		
	Long	100	contracts
	Short	50	contracts
		50	net
Requirement	(times)	$ 1,000	per contract
		$ 50,000	deposit

Illustration G-2

This term may also refer to all requirements of a customer account when margining for exchange purposes.

See: *Net Margining*

Gross Position

The accounting of both long and short positions being held in any one trading month of a commodity rather than netting those positions within one customer account. Gross position reporting is required by the clearing house to account for calculating the commodity open interest (commitment) and delivery handling.

Domestic omnibus accounts must be maintained and reported on a gross basis. Other types of accounts are netted when long and short positions are open on the same contract month. However, different customers may not be netted to each other even if in the same contract month.

Example:

Omnibus account: representing 3 customers having open positions in May Cocoa

	Long	Short	
Customer 1	2		
Customer 2	3	5	
Customer 3		4	
	5	9	gross positions

Hedge account: maintains a position in May Cocoa as a wait and instruct account

	Long	Short	
March 4	3		
March 20	4		
April 15	3		
May 5		5	
	10	less 5 = 5 net long positions	

Note: In the hedge account illustration, the position would be reported as gross (10 by 5) when it is known that the 5 shorts are hedges and not liquidations awaiting instructions.

Speculating account: restricted from remaining long and short the same contract month except if there is a sale for retender.

Clearing broker account: represents 5 clients long 100 May Cocoa and 2 clients short 25 May Cocoa. (Assume none are omnibus.)

	Long	*Short*	
5 clients	100		net
2 clients		25	net
	100	25	gross positions

Gross Processing Margin

See: *GPM*

Gross Profit

The amount of profit gained from buying and selling something, before commissions and fees are calculated.

Example:

		Total Value
Sold 1 Oct Cotton @ 7710	=	$38,550.00
Bought 1 Oct Cotton @ 7695	=	38,475.00
Gross Profit		$ 75.00
Commissions		−60.00
Net Profit		$ 15.00

See: *Net Profit*

Gross Weight

An entire weight, including package, contents, and sometimes carrier.

Example: Gross weight of a truckload of frozen pork bellies at a highway weigh-in station:

Frozen pork bellies	38,000 lbs
Cartons	600 lbs
Truck weight (unloaded)	40,000 lbs

Gross weight may be stated

Gross weight of shipment	= 78,600 lbs
Gross weight of bellies	= 38,000 lbs
Gross weight of packaged bellies	= 38,600 lbs

See: *Net Weight*

GTC

See: *Good Til Cancelled*

Guarantee Fund

A pool of liquid assets deposited by the clearing members and held at the clearing house independent of daily settlements. These funds are the initial reserve drawn upon in case of financial failure by a clearing member.

Guaranty

A written, formal contract among three parties: a *grantor* promises to pay or perform a given service to a *creditor* or benefitor of the contract if a *grantee* fails to fulfill stated terms.

Something given or taken as security to insure that a promise will be fulfilled.

Guided Account

An account that participates with similar accounts in a program directed by a mutual administrator. The administrator plans the trading strategies and manages the accounting. The client is advised to enter and/or liquidate specific trading positions. However, approval to enter the order must be given by the client.

These programs usually require a minimum initial investment and include a trading strategy that will utilize only a part of the investment at any given time. The administrator is compensated by commissions, a monthly management fee, or both.

Halfturn

A method of compensation. The salesperson receives production credit for half the commission at the initial buy or sell and the other half with the offsetting trade.

See: *Roundturn*

Hand Signals

A standardized, accepted series of arm and hand positions used to relay messages on the trading floor. These signals enable brokers to communicate despite the roar of the pit.

> **Example:** Most common, and used almost universally, is the buyer raising the hand with the palm in toward the face.
>
> The seller does the opposite, showing the palm out with the back of the hand towards the face.
>
> Some signals with fingers held vertically indicate the number of contracts the trader wishes to buy or sell at the price indicated.
>
> Some signals with combinations of fingers held vertically signify the months traded.
>
> Holding the arm and fingers in a horizontal position, the trader shows with finger signals the price above or below the last sale he/she wishes to trade. The trades shown in Illustration H-1 are as follows:

Fist	1 full cent
4 fingers extended and together	¾ cent
4 fingers extended and apart	½ cent
2 fingers extended and apart	¼ cent

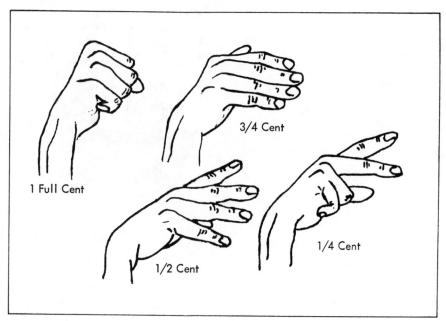

Illustration H-1

Hard Currency

Metal and/or paper processed by minting and printing into recognized values of exchange to be used by a nation as its money medium.

Assets other than money (government issues, credit cards) that are accepted in lieu of cash for payment.

Money under a banking policy of restricted credit, high interest rates, and other limitations on speculative investment or unnecessary spending.

Also known as: *Hard Money*

See: *Soft Currency*

Hard Money

See: *Hard Currency*

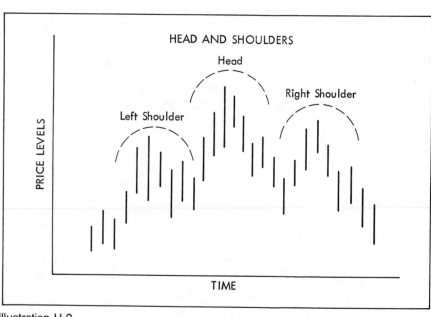

Illustration H-2

| | **Haircut** | A discount. |

Haircut

A discount.

Head and Shoulders

On a bar chart, a basic price-pattern formation resembling a left shoulder, head, and right shoulder, which is used by analysts as an indication of a significant reversal period. The formation may be upright or inverted, depending on the market. See Illustration H-2.

Heavy Market

Any market in which prices are declining.

Hedge

The establishment of a futures or option contract that represents a temporary substitute for a transaction to be made at a later time in the physical (cash) market. The transaction is appropriate when used to reduce the risk of price movement (decline/advance) or positioning for anticipated future requirements in the physical market. See Illustration H-3.

On March 23:	
Cash Market	*Futures Market*
A crop of 5,000 bushels of wheat is being grown.	Chicago July Wheat is trading at 540 per bushel.
Price objective to be sold at $5.20 per bushel.	The grower sells 1 contract at 540 as a hedge.
In July:	
The grower sells the wheat at $4.90 per bushel.	The grower buys back the short sale made in March at 510.
Calculation:	
Sale of Wheat	$4.90
Gain on futures	.30
Gross price received	$5.20

Illustration H-3

Also known as: *Price Insurance*

Note: The example does not reflect commissions or other merchandising expenses. Also, no hedge guarantees the exact prices to be received.

Hedge Letter

A document signed and dated by a customer stating the commodity in which the customer qualifies for hedge privileges. The test for qualification rests on the primary purpose of the customer's business and the relationship of the commodity to that business.

Hedge Margin

A special margin rate set by the governing exchange for accounts that qualify as bona fide hedgers, such as dealers or manufacturers. This rate is usually lower than rates offered to speculator accounts.

See: *Customer Margin/Speculator Margin*
        House Margin

Hedger

A person or entity participating in the physical commodity who holds positions in the futures and/or options in order to be protected from the risk of price fluctuations. Generally, this person produces, markets, and/or processes the commodity.

See: *Speculator*

High-Low-Close

The three primary quotations of a given day: highest trading price reached, lowest trading price, and closing price.

Example: Consider February COMEX Gold on January 4:

	High	Low	Close
	388.50	383.80	388.00

Note: For some commodities, closing price may be given as a range.

Historical Analysis

Analysis that uses past performance of prices as a basis for determining trends and prices. The analysis is generally studied over months, years, or recurring events.

See: *Cyclic Analysis*
Fundamental Analysis
Technical Analysis

Holder

See: *Buyer*

Horizontal Spread

A long option position paired for margin purposes with a short option of the same class with a different expiration.

Example:

Long 1 Dec T-bond Call @ 60
Short 1 Mar T-bond Call @ 62
Long 1 Dec T-bond Call @ 70
Short 1 Mar T-bond Call @ 68

See: *Vertical Spread*

House Account

A proprietary account of the brokerage house. This account is used to carry inventory in the products the proprietor handles. This account has nothing to do with customer activity and is maintained as a firm's own trading account.

Note: This account is considered a nonsegregated account for reporting purposes.

Example: A stock firm trades financial instrument commodities to leverage and protect capital.

A label used for a customer account that qualifies for nonsegregation on its own books. The label "House" is used for audit trail purposes.

Note: For reporting purposes, this account is considered segregated by the handling broker and nonsegregated by the customer.

House Margin

The margin deposited at the clearing house by a member to maintain its proprietary positions.

The margin required from employees, officers, or investors in a firm to maintain an open position on the books.

A level of margin set by the brokerage firm for its retail customers higher than the exchange-required minimum.

Also known as: *Speculator Margin (Rate)*

See: *Customer Margin/Speculator Margin*
Hedge Margin

ID Entry

The standard abbreviation for *Immediate Delivery Entry*. An import customs entry document which expedites the clearance of cargo by allowing delivery of cargo prior to payment of estimated duty and processing of the consumption entry. (Up to ten days are allowed for payment of duties and filing of consumption entry.)

IMF

The standard abbreviation for the *International Monetary Fund*, an international organization headquartered in Washington, D.C. and set up to aid in creating a freer system of world trade. Consisting of 126 member nations, this organization helps to achieve economic growth, higher employment, and better standards of living. The members cooperate to stabilize exchange rates and maintain orderly exchange arrangements.

Immediate Delivery Entry

See: *ID Entry*

Immediate Order

See: *Fill or Kill/FOK*

Immediate Transportation Entry

An import customs entry document that allows cargo to be moved from a pier to an inland destination without payment of duties or entry finalizations.

Also known as: *IT Entry*

Import

Goods shipped into a buying country from the originating country.

The procurement of those goods.

See: *Export*

Import Document

A written instrument that furnishes information or serves as evidence, proof, or support of imported goods: for example, an arrival notice, freight release, or customs entry.

See: *Export Document*

Import Duty	A tax levied by a country on goods brought in from another country (location). **See:** *Export Duty*
Import License	A government-issued document authorizing and regulating the importation of goods. **See:** *Export License*
Import Quota	A limitation placed by a government on the types and quantities of goods eligible for importation. **See:** *Export Quota*
Inactive Account	An account with few or no transactions but with a ledger balance. An account sitting idle, with no positions or ledger balance.
In-and-Out-Trade	**See:** *Day Trade*
Inconvertible (currency)	Currency that is not exchangeable for its equivalent value in gold or silver. The acceptability is based on the stability of the issuing government. **Example:** U.S. dollars. **Note:** Prior to 1934, U.S. paper could be redeemed at face value for gold.
Index	A price-averaged group of related products that is recognized and accepted as an economic barometer. **Example:** Standard & Poor's 500 (companies) Gas and electric Transportation
Index (Option)	A contract to buy or sell a call or a put on a group of related products or services reflecting the general market conditions at a fixed (average) price for a given period of time. Value (price) is based on the futures price relationship to strike price and the length of time remaining before expiration of the option. **Example:** S & P 500 Stock Index NYSE Composit Index **See:** *Subindex (Option)*
Inflation	Increase in the volume of money and/or credit in relation to the availability of goods, resulting in rising prices.
Initial Margin	Cash or securities required as a good-faith deposit to establish a specific, new position in the futures or option market. An initial margin amount is set by the respective exchange. **Note:** Initial margin is not a partial payment of the purchase. **Also known as:** *Original Margin, Opening Margin, Security Deposit* **See:** *Maintenance Margin/Variation Margin*
Initial Margin Call	The demand to deposit initial margin.

The instrument or document issued by a futures commission merchant to a customer specifying the deposit required to carry a given position.

Also known as: *Original Margin Call*

See: *Maintenance Margin Call/Variation Margin Call*

Inland Bill (of Exchange)

A bill of exchange drawn in one state (or location) of a given country and payable in another location of that state.

A bill of exchange drawn in a specified country and payable in another location of the country.

See: *Foreign Bill (of Exchange)*

Inland Bill of Lading

A bill, also known by the standard abbreviation *pro*, that documents the transportation of goods between point of origin and destination. This detailed document may be matched to a dock receipt.

Also known as: *Waybill (on rail), Proforma bill of lading (in trucking), Proticket.*

Inside Information

Market statistical data, financial reports, rule changes, or news events intended for public distribution that have not been released. Person(s) in possession of such material are restricted from profiting on its use until distribution has been made.

Example:
Criteria that may affect market performance and/or prices may be available to government employees and officials involved in accumulating and developing statistical reports or studies on acreage, production, usage, and so on.

Privileged financial information and upcoming rule changes are available to exchange personnel and committee members.

Insider Trading

The practice of participating in transactions based on privileged information (information gained by one's position and not available to the public). Insider trading is illegal when such transactions affect the price, giving an unfair advantage to the trader.

Inspection

A physical examination of contract samples or the entire deliverable quantity to determine that the contract standards are met.

Example:
Coffee—sample from several bags
Cotton—sampling of each bale
Livestock—inspection of livestock in the pen

Instruct

A method of selecting or matching offsetting positions in which the client specifies the position(s) and time of offset.

Example: *Speculative Account—*

Open position on the morning of January 17:

Jan 13 Long 5M May Wheat @ 345
Jan 13 Long 5M May Wheat @ 346
Jan 16 Long 10M May Wheat @ 347

Traded on January 17:

Sold 5M May Wheat @ 349

On January 17, the account instructs the broker to offset the sell with the January 13 long at 346. Complete information must be given to insure proper offset.

A privilege extended to hedge or omnibus accounts where both longs and shorts for the same commodity and month are permitted and liquidated upon instruction of the client. This privilege is addressed in the Commodity Futures Trading Commission regulations.

Example: *Hedge or omnibus account—*

Open position as of April 1 in Sugar #11:

	Long				Short		
Mar	4	4	@ 398	Mar	6	9	@ 400
Mar	5	1	@ 396	Mar	7	5	@ 398
Mar	6	4	@ 395	Mar	11	1	@ 405
Mar	8	3	@ 400	Mar	11	1	@ 404
Mar	14	2	@ 410	Mar	11	3	@ 406
		14				19	

The above account may instruct to liquidate (pair off) any number of equal (quantities) longs versus shorts to the total of the lesser side. (A maximum of 14 may be liquidated.)

Also known as: *Wait and Instruct*

An account that uses this method of selection.

The trades within this type of account.

See: *FIFO*
Reference Trade
Special vs. (Trade)

Insurance

See: *Assurance*

Insurance Certificate

An export document that assures consignment of protection to cover losses or damage (of transit cargo).

Insurance Policy

See: *Assurance*

Insured

See: *Assured*

Insurer

In an insurance contract, the party who receives payment of a premium and in return offers financial protection against damage or loss of specified item(s).

Also known as: *Underwriter*

Interbank Market

A communication network linking banks, foreign exchange brokers, and corporations for the execution of spot and forward currency transactions.

Also known as: *FX (Forward) Market*

Intercommodity Spread

The purchase and sale of two different, but related, commodities with the same delivery month and trading on the same exchange.

Also known as: *Interproduct Spread*

Example:

Chicago Board of Trade

Long 5M May Wheat
Short 5M May Oats

Chicago Mercantile Exchange

Long 4 Apr Hogs
Short 3 Apr Cattle

Note: In the example, the Chicago Mercantile Exchange specifies differing given quantities, as well as the commodities necessary to qualify as a spread.

See: *Interdelivery Spread/Intermonth Spread/Intracommodity Spread*
Spread

Intercrop Spread

The purchase and sale of the same commodity on the same exchange with one position in one crop year and the other in another crop year. This spread exists only in raw agricultural commodities. See Illustration I-1.

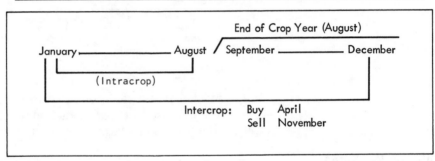

Illustration I-1

See: *Intracrop Spread*
Spread

Intercurrency Spread

The purchase and sale of two different currencies.

Example:

International Monetary Market (CME)

Long 1 Jan Swiss francs
Short 1 Jan Deutsche marks

Interday Call

A variation margin call requested during the trading session against positions known to be held at the close of the previous day.

Example: Today is February 17

Market Open	9:00 a.m. to 3:00 p.m.
February 16	Position on close 20 longs
February 17	Bought 10 (position at this moment 30 long)
February 17	1:00 p.m. issued call on 20 longs

Note: The call is issued before the market closes and trades executed on February 17 are not considered.

Interdelivery Spread

The purchase and sale of two different delivery months of the same commodity on the same exchange.

Also known as: *Intracommodity Spread or Intermonth Spread*

Example:

New York Commodity Exchange (COMEX)
Long 1 Dec Gold
Short 1 Feb Gold

See: *Spread*

Interest

A sum of money paid or received for the use of money.

A legal right to or ownership in something.

Interest-Rate Parity

A basic theorem used by arbitrageurs, which states that at equilibrium, the currency of a higher-interest-rate country will sell at a forward rate discounted in terms of a lower-interest-rate country's currency or the lower-interest-rate country currency forward will sell at a premium.

Example:

July 3 90-day Certificates of Deposit	
Interest Rate U.S.	5%
England	10%
Differential	5%

At interest-rate parity, one year forward rates for the pound should sell at a 5% discount. Variations from equilibrium may be a trigger for an arbitrageur to participate in the market.

Intermarket Spread

The purchase and sale of the same commodity on two different exchanges.

Example:

Chicago Board of Trade (CBT)
Long 5 Mar Silver (1,000 oz. each)

New York Commodity Exchange (COMEX)
Short 1 Mar Silver (5,000 oz.)

See: *Spread*

Intermediate Crop

The period for products harvested throughout the year, which is after or between the primary crop seasons.

Example:
Three quarters of the year's cocoa is harvested during October through March, the main season. Production also takes place during May through September, the Mid Crop season.

This term is also used to describe the crops produced during this season.

Lastly, a major harvest which occurs outside the main crop geographical area but at the same time of major production.

Also known as: *Mid Crop*

See: *Main Crop*

Intermonth Spread

See: *Interdelivery Spread/Intercommodity Spread*

| Interproduct Spread | See: *Intercommodity Spread* |

International Commodity Agreement

An agreement between given basic-commodity-producing nations to set a common market position in limiting production and/or setting prices.

> **Example:**
> OPEC (Organization of Petroleum Exporting Countries)

International Monetary Fund

See: *IMF*

International Payments Agreement

An agreement between two or more nations that specifies the terms of payments due between them (goods and/or currency).

Interstate Carrier

A carrier operating in more than one state, territory, or possession and thus under federal regulation and jurisdiction.

See: *Intrastate Carrier*

Interstate Commerce

Commerce carried on in two or more states, territories, or possessions and thus under federal regulation and jurisdiction.

See: *Intrastate Commerce*

In-the-Money

An expression of the relationship of an option to the underlying futures contract. For a call, both long and short, the current price of the underlying futures is higher than the strike price of the option. For a put, both long and short, the current price of the underlying futures is lower than the strike price of the option. This relationship may be a factor in determining margin requirements.

> **Example:** Consider COMEX Gold February. The futures settlement is 400. Options are as follows:

Strike	Call	Put
380	10.00	2.00
400	1.30	13.30
420	.20	32.20

Calls, both long and short, trading at a strike of 380 are considered in-the-money. Puts, both long and short, trading at a strike of 420 are considered in-the-money.

To determine the amount an option is in-the-money:

In-the-money = (difference between futures settlement and strike price) × factor × quantity

In the example, one call, either long or short, at 380 would be

Futures Settlement		Strike Price		Factor		Qty		
(400	−	380)	×	100	×	1	=	$2,000.00

In the example, one put, either long or short, at 420 would be

Strike Price		Futures Settlement		Factor		Qty		
(420	−	400)	×	100	×	1	=	$2,000.00

In-the-money may be a positive or negative amount. A long option in-the-money is a credit reflecting the theoretical profit to the holder of the option if the option is exercised. A short option in-the-money is a debit reflecting the theoretical loss to the grantor of the option if the option is assigned.

See: *At-the-Money*
Intrinsic Value
Out-of-the-Money

Intracommodity Spread

See: *Interdelivery Spread/Intermonth Spread*

Intracrop Spread

The purchase and sale of the same commodity on the same exchange with both positions lying within one crop year. See Illustration I-2.

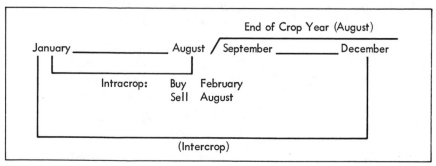

Illustration I-2

See: *Intercrop Spread/Intermonth/Intracommodity Spread*
Spread

Intramarket Spread

The purchase of a commodity and sale of the same commodity of a different contract month or of a different commodity of the same or a different month, both contracts of which are trading on the same exchange.

Example:

Chicago Board of Trade
Long 5M May Wheat
Short 5M July Wheat

See: *Intercommodity Spread*
Intracommodity spread/Interdelivery Spread/Intermonth Spread
Spread

Intrastate Carrier

A carrier operating entirely within one state and thus under the regulations and jurisdiction of that state.

See: *Interstate Carrier*

Intrastate Commerce

Commerce carried on entirely within one state and thus under the regulations and jurisdiction of that state.

See: *Interstate Commerce*

Intrinsic Value

The absolute value of the in-the-money amount; that is, the amount that would be realized if an in-the-money option is exercised. For a call, intrinsic value is the dollar amount that the futures price is above the strike price of the option. For a put, it is the dollar amount that the futures price is below the strike price of the option.

Example: Consider COMEX Gold February:

	Option Strike Price	Futures Settlement
	380	
	400	400.00
	420	

In the above example, it is currently profitable for a holder of a long call at 380 to exercise; it is currently profitable for the holder of a long put at 420 to exercise.

	CALL		PUT	
Futures	400.00	*Option*	420
Option	380	*Futures*	400.00
Points	2000 gain	*Points*	2000 gain

Should the futures settlement rise to 420, the put would yield neither profit nor loss.

Futures Price	420.00	
Option Strike	420	
Points	-0-	(no difference)

At 440, the option becomes unprofitable to exercise.

Futures Price	440.00
Option Strike	420
Points	2000 loss

The reverse is true of the call; as the futures settlement rises, so does profitability for the holder of the long call.

Note: Premium and transaction costs are not included in determining intrinsic value but are necessary to determine actual profitability of the option at exercise.

Introducing Broker

An independent broker who solicits an account and presents that account to another broker for accounting processing. The introducing broker retains advisory rights. The carrying broker provides the accounting and documentation for the customer. Both brokers participate in the commissions earned.

Example: Broker A agrees with customer C to advise and execute all trades and arranges to have broker B process the trades and provide customer C with all accountings, confirmations, and monthly statements.

The documentation received by customer C from broker B will usually have an overprint stating "Compliments of broker A."

Inventory

A list of articles, usually including descriptions and quantities.

The process of listing or recording these articles.

The value of goods of a business.

Inventory Control

The process of accounting for goods in and out of inventory.

Inventory Valuation

The method of assessing an inventory's monetary value.

See: *FIFO*
LIFO

| **Inverted Market** | **See:** *Backwardation* |
| | *Contango/Normal Market* |

| **Invoice** | A document showing accounting, inventory, and customer billing information for products being received or delivered. Invoices may represent original details or adjustments and cancellations. |

| **Irrevocable** | Something considered permanent; not to be rescinded or cancelled. |
| | **See:** *Revocable* |

| **IT Entry** | **See:** *Immediate Transportation Entry* |

Jobber

Someone who buys goods in bulk from a manufacturer, producer, or importer and sells to a retailer. Originally, this term referred to someone who purchased in job lots or odd lots.

Also known as: *Wholesaler or Middleman*

Jobber Trade

The buy, sell, and subsequent liquidation of the same number of contracts for delivery in the same month, all executed on the same trade date. This terminology is used in the London market and corresponds to *day trade* in the United States.

See: *Day Trade*

Job Lot

A defined and unchanging quantity of a commodity smaller than the standard specification size. This unit is still recognized and permitted by the given exchange.

Example:

Mid-American mini contract		
(Job lot)	1M	Wheat
(Standard contract)	5M	Wheat

A quantity moved through commerce larger or smaller than the standard contract size.

Example: A commodity wholesales in multiples of 100 boxes.

(Standard)	100 boxes
(Job lot)	134 boxes
(Job lot)	96 boxes

Also known as: *Odd Lot*

See: *Round Lot*

Joint Account

An account held by two or more parties. The account holders join their resources and share the profits and losses of the trading activity.

A joint account may consist of related or unrelated individuals.

Example:

Related:	Husband and wife; father and son (marital/blood relationship sharing the same household)
Unrelated:	Mr. Jones and Mr. Smith (business/friend relationship)

Joint Contract

A contract obligation undertaken by two or more parties.

Joint Float

An agreement between two or more countries to stabilize their currencies in relation to each other; thereby each currency will rise and/or fall proportionate to the other.

Joint Rate

A shipping cost quoted as one amount but actually representing costs between two points by two or more carriers.

Example:

Cost to ship from Seattle, Washington, to New York, New York	$48.00
Carrier A moves cargo from Seattle to Chicago, Illinois, for	$30.00
Carrier B moves the cargo from Chicago to New York	$18.00
Total Cost	$48.00

Joint Venture

A business undertaking entered into by two or more parties and generally limited to a single goal or accomplishment.

Journal

A record or log of original entries. A journal may be used to facilitate later posting to books of final entry, such as a ledger.

Journal Entry

A written entry in which transactions are recorded or logged completely enough for accounting purposes.

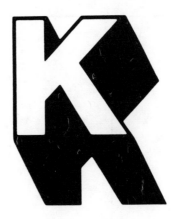

Kerb Trade

A trade that takes place after the official close of the exchange. Originally, a trade that took place on the street or in the local pub.

Kerb trade is currently associated with the London markets.

Note: This transaction is illegal in the United States.

Key Reversal

On a chart, the pivotal point of a trend change. This pattern occurs after a significant advancement or decline of a market with little or no resistance. On a day, usually one of high volume, that the market makes a new high (or low) and closes lower (or higher) than the previous day's close, it is analyzed technically as a reversal. Another element is that the reversal day usually has a high volume and may incur a noticeable open interest charge. See Illustration K-1.

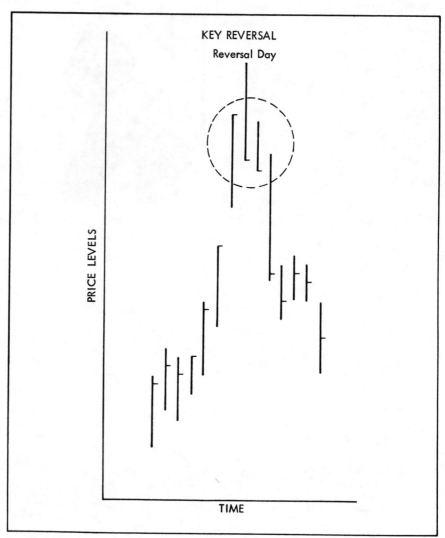

Illustration K-1

Last Delivery Day

The final day on which the long can receive delivery and the short must make delivery of the actual commodity to remain in compliance with the specifications and rules of the exchange.

Last In, First Out

The standard abbreviation for the term *last in, first out*, LIFO signifies a method of selection and matching in offsetting positions in which a given buy or sell offsets the latest trade date of the given commodity month sell or buy on file for the given customer.

> **Example:** Open positions for account ABC:

		Long		
Mar 1	2	Dec Gold	@ 402.00
Mar 3	2	Dec Gold	@ 400.00
Mar 9	3	Dec Gold	@ 397.00
Mar 10	1	Dec Gold	@ 395.00

On March 11 account ABC sells:

3 Dec Gold @ 400.00

If the customer elects a LIFO offset, the sell would select the last three positions to be held in the account (the March 10 buy at 395.00 and two of the March 9 buys at 397.00).

An account using this method of trade selection.

> **Example:** In the above Account ABC is a LIFO account.

A trade transaction using this method of selection.

> **Example:** The buy and sell offset is called a LIFO transaction.

A method of inventory valuation in which the latest goods received are the first goods sold. The last shipment determines current valuation and cost.

See: *FIFO*
       Instruct

Last Tender Day

The last day a notice of intention to deliver may be issued, as determined by contract specifications.

Last Trading Day

The one day set by the exchange on which trading ceases for a given contract. Open positions cannot be satisfied via liquidations after this date. This day is always a business day. Time for trading to cease is set by the exchange and is within normal trading hours. Futures contracts not yet offset can be settled after last trading day only by making delivery of the commodity. Option contracts not yet offset or exercised are settled after last trading day by abandonment.

Lay-down Costs

Costs incurred in the transportation of a commodity.

Also known as: *LDC*

Example:
Loading
Demurrage
Insurance
Unloading
Tariffs

LCL

The standard abbreviation for *Less Than Carload*, LCL refers to a shipment that occupies less than a full railroad car.

LDC

See: *Lay-down Costs*

Lead Month

The most current contract month in which a delivery may be made or received. See Illustration L-1.

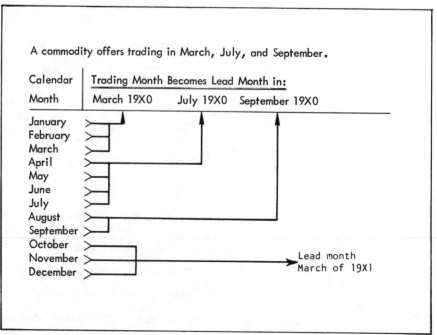

Illustration L-1

Leg

One side of a spread.

Legging Out

The execution of one leg (side) of a straddle with the trader at risk to execute the remaining leg (side).

Example:

Enter Straddle Order:	Sell	Mar
	Buy	May at 20 points
		May over
Market Situation:	Mar	trading at 400
	May	offered at 425

The broker sells March at 400, executing the sell leg (side) of the order, and bids May at 420, anticipating a seller. Until the bid is satisfied, the sale at 400 is exposed to market price risk.

Also known as: *Leg Up, Lifting a Leg*

Leg Up

The action of buying or selling one leg (side) of a straddle separately rather than obtaining both as a unit at one time.

Example: January 13,

10:00 a.m.:
Bought 1 Feb Pork Belly

2:15 p.m.:
Sold 1 Apr Pork Belly

During the time from 10:00 a.m. until the April sale at 2:15 p.m., the trader holds only one leg (side) of the straddle and assumes the full market risk on the long position.

Also known as: *Legging Out*

The liquidation of one leg (side) of an existing straddle position, leaving the remaining leg (side) exposed to market fluctuation and risk.

Example: January 13, open position of account ABC:

Long 1 Feb Gold (spread with)
Short 1 Apr Gold

On January 23 the account gives instruction to liquidate (offset) the February long with an order to:

Sell 1 Feb Gold Market

The January 13 April short for Gold remains as an open position for the account. The short is at complete risk.

Less Than Carload

See: *LCL*

Less Than Truckload

A shipment which occupies less than a full motor truck.

Also known as: *LTT*

Letter Of Credit

A financial instrument drawn by a bank on behalf of its customer. The bank guarantees payment on demand to the holder of the instrument. The bank's customer pays a fee for the credit based on the amount and time period of the instrument. The bank acts as a grantor, but the customer provides sufficient collateral. This document may be revocable or irrevocable.

| Leverage | Increased financial power gained by committing a small amount of money (margin) to control a large position (contract), generally resulting in large profits or losses. |

Leverage Contract

A specific type of contract in which the customer contracts for a long-term purchase of a commodity, such as gold or silver, from a leverage firm permitted by law to sell such instruments. The customer makes an initial payment that is a percentage of the spot price value of the commodity. A periodic charge is made against the customer for a carrying cost or fee on the unpaid balance. A leverage contract is a standardized contract but is not traded on a registered commodity exchange. The price is set by the leverage firm, not public auction.

See: *Long Leverage*
Short Leverage

Liability

The purchase and expense obligations connected with a commodity contract.

The amount owed by a debtor to a creditor.

Licensed Warehouse

A depository designated by a given exchange for delivery against a futures contract.

Lien

A claim against property.

Life of the Contract

The period of time during which trading can take place, beginning in a particular calendar month and expiring in or at the delivery month, as specified in the commodity contract.

Example: March Wheat of the current year may begin trading in October, 17 months before delivery. See Illustration L-2.

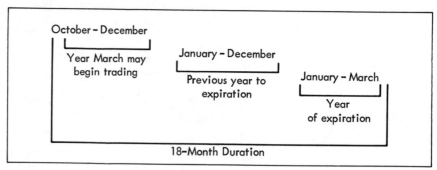

Illustration L-2

Note: In this illustration, the last seven business days in March are excluded for trading March contracts. Rules for trading vary by commodity.

Sometimes used to refer to the time already passed in which trading occurred.

Example: March Wheat may have begun trading in January of the previous year. If February is the current calendar month, then the actual contract life has been 14 months. See Illustration L-3.

LIFO

See: *Last In/First Out*

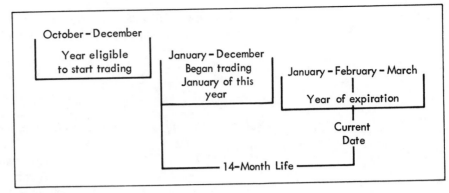

Illustration L-3

Lifting a Leg	**See:** *Legging Out*

Limit

A boundary.

See: *Basis Point*
Maximum Price Fluctuation (price limits)
Position Limit
Trading Limit
Variable Limits

Limit Day

A day on which one or more contracts close at the maximum allowable variation from the previous day's price.

Limit Down

The maximum price decline allowable in a trading session for a given commodity and contract month. A contract's daily price limit is defined in the contract detail rules and reflects one day's move.

> **Example:** Chicago-traded corn is permitted to decline or advance 10c from the previous day's settlement price. If

Monday Mar Corn closed at	3.20
Tuesday Mar Corn can close at	3.10
Maximum allowable decline	.10

Note: The contract market allows for an additional mechanism when contract daily limit moves are inadequate.

See: *Limit Move*
Limit Up
Variable Limits

Limited Risk

An investment for which maximum loss can be predetermined.

> **Example:** The premium paid for an option is the maximum loss that may occur on that transaction. The risk is limited.

Purchase premium is	$500.00
Option expires or declines to zero	-0-
Total risk is limited to	$500.00

Limited Risk Spread

A spread consisting of purchasing a near month of a given commodity and selling the distant month at premium; the difference between the spread and the full carrying charge (storage, interest, insurance) is the risk.

Example: On December 1 an elevator operator buys 5,000 bushels of wheat that is expected to be resold in March.

Cash Market	Long 5M	Wheat @ 340
Futures	Short 5M	Mar Wheat @ 355

The risk is 15¢ per bushel, or 5¢ carrying charge per month per bushel.

Note: This theory is limited to a storable commodity.

Limit Move

The maximum price advance or decline allowable in a trading session for a given commodity and contract month. A contract's daily price limit is defined in the contract detail rules and reflects one day's move.

See: *Limit Down*
Limit Up

Limit Only

In trading, the definite price specified by a client restricting the broker as to the price level at which an order may be executed. The stated price is to buy at not more than or sell for not less than.

See: *Limit Order*

Limit Order

An order with some restriction(s), such as price, time, or both, on execution. Restrictions are set by the client.

Example: *Time limit—*

Buy 1 Apr Gold @ 400.00 Opening Only

may also be written as

B 1 J GLD @ 400.00 Opening Only

Example: *Price limit—*

Buy 1 Apr Gold @ 390.00

may also be written as

B 1 J GLD @ 390.00

See: *Market Order*

Limit Up

The maximum price advance allowable in a trading session for a given commodity and contract month. The contract daily price limit is defined in the contract detail rules and reflects one day's move.

Example: Chicago-traded corn is permitted to decline or advance 10¢ from the previous day's settlement price. If

Monday Mar Corn closed at	3.20
Tuesday Mar Corn can close at	3.30
Maximum allowable advance	.10

Note: The contract markets allow for an additional mechanism when contract daily limits prove inadequate.

See: *Limit Down*
Limit Move
Variable Limits

Line of Credit

See: *Credit Line*

Liquidation

To close out or offset a previously established long position.

Example: A customer is

Long 5 Feb Gold @ 400.00

Today the customer

Sells 5 Feb Gold @ 420.00

The sale liquidates or removes the long position.

See: *Cover*

Sometimes used interchangeably with *close-out* or *offset* in regard to finalizing either a long or short.

See: *Close-out/Offset*

Liquidity

That which is readily convertible into cash.

Example:
Listed securities

An easy flow of trades.

Example:
A market having many buyers and sellers within a narrow price range

Liquid Market

A market condition in which a large number of participants are buying and selling substantial quantities at small price differences, thereby creating easy trading opportunities.

Loan Value

The amount granted an in-the-money long option to satisfy a variation margin call of an offsetting futures position. This value is considered "secured" because the amount is self-liquidating (liquidation should be profitable).

Example: February 4:

Long Option 1 Apr Gold Call @ 400
Short Futures 1 Apr Gold   @ 420.00
Settlement Price on Futures   450.00

When the futures position (short) is marked to the market, variation margin may appear to be due; however, loan value from the in-the-money option (long) may be applied.

Loan Value = (Difference between Strike Price and Futures Settlement) × factor × quantity

Formula for loan value:

Futures Settlement	Strike Price	Factor	Qty	
(450.00	− 400) ×	100 ×	1	or
(450.00 − 400.00) =	50.00 ×	100 ×	1	= $5,000.00

Market Value of Futures	$45,000.00
Short Value of Sale (futures)	42,000.00
Variation Margin Due	$ 3,000.00
Loan Value Available (option)	5,000.00

Loan Value in excess, no margin due.

Local (Broker)

A floor broker who may trade for customers but primarily for his or her own account, continuously buying and selling for quick profits.

Also known as: *Scalper*

See: *Floor Trader/Market Maker*

Long

A commitment that has been bought and is awaiting final sale or delivery.

The party who has bought and is holding a futures or options contract or owns an actual commodity that has not been settled by sale or delivery.

The party who is buying a position that does not have an offsetting sale established in the account.

See: *Short*

Long Leverage

A transaction in which a customer contracts to buy a metal from a leverage firm by putting down a partial payment and making payments to that firm.

See: *Short Leverage*

LTT

See: *Less Than Truckload*

Main Crop

The harvest time of largest production. This harvest fulfills the bulk needs of domestic and export calendar-year requirements.

> **Example:** Three-quarters of the year's cocoa is harvested during October through March.

Crops or products grown during this time.

See: *Intermediate Crop/Mid Crop*

Maintenance Level

The monetary value to which the original margin requirement may depreciate and still be considered satisfactory margin to carry the established position. A minimum is specified by the governing exchange, but it may be the policy of an individual firm to set a minimum higher than the governing exchange's.

Also known as: *Variation Allowance*

Example:

Initial Requirement 1 Contract	$4,000.00
Allowable Market Fluctuation (negative)	−1,000.00
Maintenance Level for the Contract	$3,000.00

Note: The rule of thumb is maintenance at 75% of the original requirement.

Maintenance Margin

Additional margin required on an established position due to depreciation in the value of the contract.

Also known as: *Variation Margin*

Example:

Maintenance Level 75%

		No Call		On Call
Requirement		$4,000		$4,000
Market Fluctuation (negative)		1,000	(25%)	1,001*
		$3,000		$2,999

*A call is issued for $1,001.00 because the market has depreciated more than 25%.

Note: Issuance of the margin call is a requirement of all exchanges.

See: *Initial Margin/Original Margin*

Maintenance Margin Call

The demand to deposit funds to restore an account to the required level.

The instrument or document issued by a futures commission merchant to a customer that specifies the deposit required.

Also known as: *Variation Margin Call*

See: *Initial Margin Call/Original Margin Call*

Maker

The original signer of a promissory note. The maker is the borrower and is responsible for payment.

Managed Account

See: *Controlled Account/Discretionary Account*

Manifest

An itemized listing of a carrier's cargo, showing origin, destination, consignee(s), physical characteristics of the cargo, etc.

Manipulation

The control of market factors for one's own profit, such as a commodity cartel or governmental control of monetary policy. Manipulation is undertaken to maintain prices artificially rather than by supply and demand.

Margin

Cash, securities, or their equivalent, required as a performance bond to carry a given commodity contract.

Also known as: *(Margin) Requirement*

> **Example:** Depending on the various exchanges, deposits can be cash, U.S. government obligations, listed securities, letters of credit, and warehouse receipts.

See: *Initial Margin/Original Margin/Security Deposit Maintenance Margin/Variation Margin*

Margin Call

A demand either to deposit initial margin (at contract initiation) or to restore margin to a specified level during the duration of a commodity contract.

Margin Requirement

See: *Margin*

Market

Trade or commerce in a commodity.

A place where commodities are publicly bought and sold.

Market Appreciation

The increase in value of a position from one day to the next.

Also known as: *Market Improvement*

Example: On March 2 a trader owns

Position	Trade Price	Settlement Price
Long 1 Apr Gold	420.00	420.00

On March 3 the market advances to 422.00. The position held on March 2 has improved or appreciated:

March 3 Settlement Price	422.00
March 2 Trade Price (long)	420.00
Market Appreciated	2.00

Settlement Price		Trade Price		Factor		Qty		Value
(422.00	−	420.00)	×	10	×	1	=	$200.00

The market has appreciated $200.00.

Market Basis Order

A contingency buy or sell order to be executed based on another contract.

Example:

Buy 5M July Wheat Market Basis May 360

may also be written as

B 5M N WHT MKT Basis K 360

In this order, July Wheat will be purchased at whatever the market is trading at *when and if* May Wheat reaches 360.

Market if Touched

A contingency order given with a limited price instruction that when the market reaches the required price level, becomes a market order to trade at the next best trading price.

This term is also known by the standard abbreviation *MIT*.

Example:

Buy 1 Dec Gold @ 320.00 Market if Touched

may also be written as

B 1 Z GLD @ 320.00 MIT

This buy order is placed below the marker and is not to be executed unless and until the market reaches 320.00. At that point, the order becomes a market order and is executed at the best available price. The 320.00 price level cannot be guaranteed. See Illustration M-1.

Note: This order can be given as a sell order as well. The significant difference between a MIT order and a Stop order is its location for execution relative to current prices.

See: *Stop Loss Order*

Market Improvement

See: *Market Appreciation*

Market Maker

See: *Floor Trader*

Market on Close (MOC)

See: *At-the-Close*

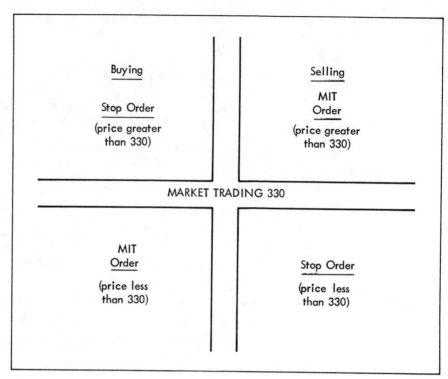

Illustration M-1

Market Order

See: *At-the-Market*

Market Price

The price at which a commodity contract is currently selling in the market place or exchange.

Market Value

The monetary value of a contract in the market place on a given day. This value is expressed as

Settlement Price × Factor × Quantity

Example: Consider the New York Composite:

Settlement Price on a Given Day	$68
Factor	500
Quantity in Contracts	1
$68 × $500 × 1 =	$34,000

On a given day 1 contract of the composite, which settled at $68, has a market value of $34,000.

Note: The factor for this commodity, 500, is a constant and does not change from day to day or with the number of contracts being traded.

See: *Face Value/Par Value*

Mark to Market

A method of calculating gains or losses on open positions with closing prices at the end of the day.

For futures, this value is established by the following calculation:

Difference between Trade Price and Settlement Price × Factor × Quantity

Example: Consider COMEX Gold:

Settlement price on Given Day	396.00
Trade Price of Given Position	396.40
Factor for Gold (per 10 cents)	$10.00
Number of Contracts for Trade	2
Settlement Price	$396.00
Trade Price	396.40
	.40 or 40 points

Points		Factor		Qty	
40	×	$10.00	×	2	= $80.00 loss if position is long.
40	×	$10.00	×	2	= $80.00 gain if position is short.

Note: The factor, $10.00 in the case of gold, is constant and does not change from day to day or with the number of contracts. In addition, note that this calculation reveals market gain or loss, not contract value.

For options, this means determining the current premium market value of the option. This is accomplished by the following calculation:

Option Settlement Price × Factor × Quantity

Example: Sugar #11:

Settlement Price on a Call @ 11.00	$ 3.05, or 305 points
Factor (per 1 cent)	$11.20
Number of Contracts for Trade	1

Points		Factor		Qty	
305	×	$11.20	×	1	= $3,416

The value of this option on this day is $3,416.

Note: The original trade price is not taken into consideration. The factor, $11.20 in the case of Sugar #11, is constant and does not change from day to day or with the number of contracts.

Matching

A method of checking buys and sells to insure agreement on quantity and prices of contracts traded on a given day at the exchange.

The method by which a given trade finds and offsets another trade.

Maturity

The period during which a futures contract is settled by delivery in accordance with the contract's delivery specifications.

The date on which a financial instrument becomes due and is to be paid off.

Maximum Price Fluctuation

The exchange-specified limit or maximum amount a contract price can change up or down during a given trading session.

Example: Chicago Board of Trade T–bonds' maximum price fluctuation is (64/32nds) above or below the previous day's settlement price ($2,000.00 per contract), subject to variable limits provisions of the Exchange.

COMEX Gold is 2,500 points ($2,500.00 per contract) above or below the previous day's settlement price, subject to variable limits provisions of the Exchange.

See: *Basis Point/Minimum Price Fluctuation/Point/Tick*

Medium of Exchange	Something acceptable as money.

> **Example:**
> Coins
> Paper money
> Drafts
> Money orders

Member

See: *Clearing Member*
Exchange Member

Member Fee

A fee charged by the exchange and/or clearing house per contract for using its facilities.

Member Rate

The commission negotiated and charged for the execution of an order for a member of the exchange. The base level negotiated is lower for members and privileged accounts.

Note: Since the introduction of negotiated commissions, there is no longer an official member rate. The industry, however, continues to use the term as a label for special consideration toward exchange members.

''M'' Formation

See: *Double Top*

Mid Crop

See: *Intermediate Crop*

Mid-day Call

A demand from the clearing house for an interim margin deposit during the day. This call is necessary when market conditions are volatile.

Note: This margin call must be met within one hour of notification by the clearing house.

A mid-day call may also be exercised by brokerage houses against customers holding large positions that are losing money.

Note: These calls for settlement of margin variation do not replace normal end-of-day settlement but are taken into consideration at that time.

Minimum Equity

An exchange- or broker-imposed liquidity level that must be maintained in a certain type of account.

The customer's ledger balance (cash) with the accumulation of the trade equity, if any, must be equal to any minimum equity requirement to remain in compliance.

> **Example:** The Chicago Mercantile Exchange requires all discretionary accounts to maintain a minimum equity of $3,750. If there are no open positions in the account, a minimum of $5,000 cash balance must still be maintained or orders are not permitted.

Minimum Margin

The lowest level of good-faith deposit permitted by an exchange for one contract position in a given commodity.

Note: This rate is most commonly associated with speculative trades as hedges are generally offered a special exchange hedge rate.

Minimum Price Fluctuation

See: *Basis Point*

Minus Tick

See: *Down Tick*

MIT

See: *Market if Touched*

MOC	**See:** *At-the-Close*
Monetary Reserve	The amount of precious metal and foreign currencies held by a government to secure its obligations.
Monetary Unit	The main unit of currency of a given country. **Example:** U.S. dollar British pound
Money	A medium of exchange in the form of coins or paper currency in measured value and acceptable as payment for goods and services.
Money Market	A worldwide market trading in short-term debt obligations of governments, financial institutions, etc.
Money Supply	The total amount of currency and demand deposits (valued in that currency) available for use.
Monopoly	Such extensive ownership of a source commodity that one can control supply and price of that commodity. **Note:** One or more persons or entities conspiring together for control can create a monopoly.
Monthly Statement	An accounting statement reflecting cash and/or trade activity for the month, open positions, cash balance, and trade equity at month end. Futures-industry regulations require this document to be furnished to the client.
Moving Average	A method for averaging near-term prices in relation to long-term prices. Oldest prices are dropped as new ones are added.

Example:

Closing prices day 1	2.00
2	2.01
3	2.02
Average (6.03 divided by 3) = 2.01	

As a new day is added, the oldest is dropped.

Closing prices day 2	2.01
3	2.02
4	2.03
Average (6.06 divided by 3) = 2.02	

Note: Moving averages are not restricted to day measurements. Any constant unit measure can be applied, and the average can be of as few as two units to whatever number of units the user wishes.

Moving-Average Chart	An analysis chart that plots the points resulting from averaging prices. See Illustration M-2. (Note that in the chart, each day (point) actually represents the average of the given number of days—3, 5, 7, etc.) **See:** *Bar Chart*
Mutual Funds	An open-ended investment trust based on shares of diversified positions. Dollars are pooled from shareholders and used to purchase money assets. The selection, purchase, and sale of investments are the responsibility of the trust.

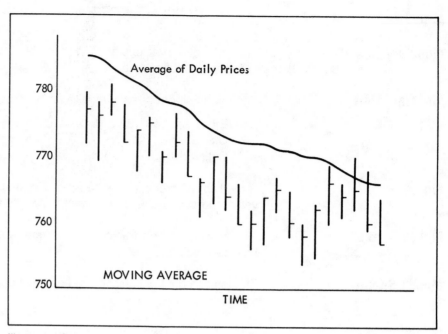

Illustration M-2

Naked

A long or short position that has no pair-off for margin or hedging purposes and is considered to stand alone.

Example:

Option Long 1 July Sugar #11 (Call)
Future Short 3 Dec Cocoa

More commonly, options written against cash or other margin rather than the underlying commodity.

Also known as: *Uncovered*

Sometimes used interchangeably with *net*.

See: *Covered Option*
Net
Spread/Straddle

Narrow Basis

A condition in which the difference between the spot and futures prices is small or the spot price is higher than the futures price, indicating short supply and high demand.

Also known as: *Strong Basis*

Example: On a given day, corn is trading at $3.08 per bushel in the cash market. (The normal basis for this example is .08¢.) Prices will tend to move up or down together but may do so in unequal amounts. If on that day, corn is trading at $3.14 per bushel in the futures market, the narrow basis is considered strong because

Futures	@ 3.14
Cash	@ 3.08
Basis	.06

basis .02 narrower than the normal .08.

See: *Weak Basis/Wide Basis*

Narrow Market	A market in which there are relatively few trades and open commitments.

Narrow Market

A market in which there are relatively few trades and open commitments.

A market in which prices move in a narrow range.

Nearby (Delivery Month)

The closest active-trading contract month for a given commodity in its futures market.

Example: Assume that the current calendar month is March:

Spot	Nearby	Deferred
March	April	May thru December, January, and February

Note: As trading can still take place in the spot month, that month is sometimes also referred to as nearby.

See: Deferred Futures (delivery month)

Negotiable

Legally transferable by delivery and/or endorsement.

Open to bargaining or conferring to come to an agreement.

See: Nonnegotiable

Negotiable Instruments

Written documents, such as orders, notes, or checks, that are unconditionally and legally transferrable via delivery and/or endorsement.

See: Nonnegotiable Instruments

Negotiable Warehouse Receipt

A warehouse receipt held by an entity that holds title to the commodity. This instrument has a value, may be endorsed to anyone, and is used to transfer ownership of the commodity. The commodity specified on the instrument is deliverable "to bearer" or to order.

See: Depository Receipt/Warehouse Receipt
  Nonnegotiable Warehouse Receipt

Negotiated Commission

A commission rate that is the result of bargaining and agreement between a broker and a customer.

Negotiated Price

A price arrived at as a result of discussion between buyer and seller.

Net

The remainder after all deductions.

See: Gross

Net Asset Value

Total asset value less total liability value of all positions held, marked to the market.

Example:

Long Position	Settlement Price	Contract Value
1 Dec COMEX Gold	@ 425.00	$42,500.00 dr
1 Dec COMEX Gold	@ 425.00	42,500.00 dr

Short Position		
1 July COMEX Gold	@ 433.00	$43,300.00 cr

Net Asset Value		
	Long Value	$85,000.00
	(less) Short Value	43,300.00
	Net Value	$41,700.00 of open position

Net Change

The difference in price from one trading day to the next (plus or minus).

Example:

Heating Oil			
Mar 2	76.50		original price
Mar 5	75.75	−.75	net point decline
Mar 6	76.00	+.25	net point advance

Note: The net point change must be multiplied by commodity factor and contract quantity to arrive at net change in dollars.

Net Loss

The result of expenditures exceeding revenue; losses exceeding profits.

Example:

	Costs Exceeding Profits	Costs plus Loss
Difference of Long and Short in Dollars	50.00 gain	50.00 loss
Commission	55.00 cost	55.00 cost
Net Loss	$ 5.00	$105.00

Net Margining

Applying margin requirements to those positions remaining after removing all possible spread combinations and netting the long and short positions of the same commodity of the same trading months.

Example:

Long 5 May Copper
Short 3 May Copper

Short 1 July Copper

Application:

1 Long May versus 1 Short July = spread margin

May position is now

4 Long and 3 Short

The 3 short May offset the 3 long May for margin purposes. The net position is long 1 May Copper, to which a margin requirement is applied.

This term is also used when referring to the requirement of a single contract.

See: Gross Margining

Net Position

A long or short position that has no pair-off within the same commodity month and is considered standing alone.

Used most commonly at the clearing house to determine the broker position susceptible to margin calculation.

Example: A clearing broker has multiple customers

	Long	Short
All Customer Positions May Copper	100	58
Subtract Lesser Amount	58	58
Broker Carriers Net Long	42	0

Note: The example is used in the same manner by the broker to determine net positions for "instruct" clients carrying long and short positions in the same commodity and contract month.

This term is sometimes used interchangeably with *naked*.

See: *Naked*

Net Price

The actual price paid after all additions, deductions, adjustments.

Net Profit

The remainder after subtracting all costs of goods, expenditures, and other deductions.

See: *Gross Profit*

Net Weight

The weight of contents, not including packaging.

See: *Gross Weight*

New Crop Year (months)

A period containing the commodity trading months of the next main crop. This period represents planting, growing, harvesting, and marketing.

Example: For soybeans, the crop year is September through August. If the current calendar month is May, the available futures contract months are

Old Crop   May, July, August
New Crop   September, November, January, March, May, July, August

See Illustration N-1.

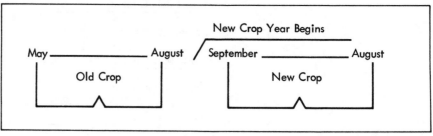

Illustration N-1

Note: The old crop and the new crop trade simultaneously, each relatively independent of the other. To distinguish old-crop August, for example, from new-crop August, the calendar year is identified at the time an order is placed.

See: *Old Crop Year (months)*

Nominal (price)

Slight or low.

An estimated price, generally established by the exchange, used in place of the closing price when there is no bid or any relevant bid, ask, or trade for the given commodity delivery month.

Noncompetitive Trades

Trades handled, executed, cleared, or carried, that are not the result of an open outcry or posting of bids and offers in the trading ring but are considered bona fide transactions.

Example:
Transfer trades
Exchange for actuals

Nonnegotiable

Lacking the ability to be freely exchanged or transferred.

Not subject to discussion.

See: *Negotiable*

Nonnegotiable Instrument

An instrument that lacks one or more prerequisites of negotiability and thus is not freely transferable.

See: *Negotiable Instrument*

Nonnegotiable Warehouse Receipt

A warehouse receipt with a blank endorsement. The financing bank holds title to the commodity. This instrument has no intrinsic value and cannot be used to move (deliver, release) the commodity.

See: *Depository Receipt/Warehouse Receipt*
Negotiable Warehouse Receipt

Nonregulated Account

A general ledger or customer account that reflects cash delivery or the accounting of commodities traded outside the borders of the U.S. and are not subject to the jurisdiction of the Commodity Futures Trading Commission.

General ledger expense and income accounts.

See: *Regulated Account*

Nonregulated Commodity

Commodities that are traded on recognized markets outside the United States and are not governed by the Commodity Futures Trading Commission.

Example:
London Raw Sugar No. 4

Also known as: *Unregulated Commodity*

See: *Regulated Commodity*

Nontraded Option

An option that can only be closed out by declaration or abandonment.

Example:

Long 6 Calls London Cocoa

Delivery	May All or None
Striking Price	12020 per tonne
Declaration Date	April 17 (10:00 a.m.)

If on April 17 the market has advanced above the strike price, the taker of the option declares the option and receives 6 lots of cocoa at 12020.

If on April 17 the market has declined, the taker abandons the option.

See: *Traded Option*

Normal Market

See: *Contango*

Not-Held Basis

A condition on an order by which a customer releases the broker of the responsibility to complete the execution of that given order.

Example:

Buy 5 May Cotton 7700 "Not Held"

The broker may not buy any of the contracts and there is no obligation to the customer. However, if the order is executed, the broker is still responsible not to pay more than the order price of 7700 on all or any part of the five lots.

A rule of an exchange limiting the responsibility of a broker to execute an order during set periods at market opening or closing.

Not-Held Order

See: *Disregard Tape Order*

Notice Day

See: *First Notice Day*

Notice of Intention to Deliver

A written notice presented by a seller to the clearing house which in turn assigns the notice and subsequent delivery of a commodity to the buyer.

Notice Period

The period of time designated by the contract rules for issuing notice of intentions. This period may be as brief as one day but never beyond the actual delivery month.

OB

The standard abbreviation for an *or better order*, an order earmarked with a specific price that may be executed at that price or a higher price (in the case of a sell) or a lower price (in the case of a buy).

Example:

Sell 5M May Wheat 330 Or Better

may also be written as

S 5M K WHT 330 OB

This order is to be executed at the given price or higher.

See: *Stop Order*

Obligation

A legally binding, enforceable agreement, contract or duty.

Ocean Bill of Lading

An export document used as a receipt for cargo and a contract for transportation. An ocean bill of lading may also be used as a negotiable instruction of ownership capable of being bought, sold, or traded while cargo is in transit.

OCO/OR

The standard abbreviation for a *One Cancels the Other order*, an order designating both sides or the same side of a trading range with different months, markets, commodities, prices, etc. When the condition of one is reached and executed, the other is cancelled.

Example:

Buy 5M July Soybeans 575 or
    5M August   579 One Cancels Other

may also be written as

B 5M N BNS 575 OR 5M Q BNS 579 OCO

This order may be executed by buying either July or August soybeans. Once either month has been purchased, the other is automatically cancelled by the broker. The choice of month traded is left to the broker, who is guided by the dictates of market conditions.

Odd Lot   **See:** *Job Lot*

Offer   **See:** *Asked*

Office Trade   **See:** *Ex-pit*

Offset   **See:** *Close-out*

For the calculation of margins, the pairing of longs and shorts of the same commodity and month in a hedge account.

Example:

Long 1 Mar 1,000 oz Silver (Chicago)
Short 2 Mar 1,000 oz Silver (Chicago)

When margins are calculated, the buy (long) contract is paired and offsets one of the sell (short) contracts, resulting in no requirement due. The remaining short is then margined as one net position.

The matching of both sides of a transaction in a clearing-broker account—the buy for one account, the sell for the same account, for reporting to the clearing house.

Old Crop Year (Months)

The period containing the commodity trading months of the current crop year when old supplies are being moved before the new harvest and new supplies are available.

Example: See Illustration O-1.

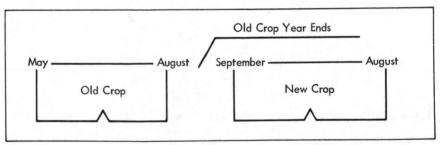

Illustration O-1

For soybeans, the crop year is September through August. If the current calendar month is May, the available futures contract months are classified thus:

Old Crop	May, July, August
New Crop	September, November, January, March, May, July, August

Note: The old crop and the new crop trade simultaneously, each relatively independent of the other. To distinguish old crop August from new crop August, the calendar year is identified at the time an order is placed.

See: *New Crop Year (Months)*

Oligopoly

A market condition in which there are so few producers or sellers that the supply (of the identical goods) offered by anyone strongly affects the market.

Omnibus Account

An account carried by one futures commission merchant with another and used for clearing purposes. The transactions flowing through an omnibus account can reflect the activities and positions of multiple customers. Since this account exists between brokers, customer identity is not of concern and the account is normally titled in the name of the introducing broker with a subtitle of *Customer Account*. The introducing broker is responsible for all margin required.

See: *Disclosed (Omnibus) Account*
Undisclosed (Omnibus) Account

On-Board Bill of Lading

An export document certifying that cargo has been placed on a specified vessel.

On Call

A purchase or sale in which the buyer (seller) agrees to a basis differential (points above or below the futures) to fix the actual cash price. The buyer (seller) may also determine the length of time before establishing the price. A futures transaction is part of the completed transaction.

See: *Buyer's Call*
Seller's Call

Note: This method of price fixing is standard in a market such as cotton. For other markets (methods),

See: *Price Fixing*

This term is also used when a holder of an open position(s) has an outstanding margin call.

Open Contract

A contract that has been bought or sold and has not been satisfied by an offsetting sale or purchase or by delivery or receipt of the commodity (in the case of a futures) or of the futures (in the case of an option).

Also known as: *Open Commitment or Open Position*

Open Commitment

See: *Open Contract*

The total number of open futures contracts (buys or sells) of a given commodity not offset by an opposite futures transaction or fulfilled by delivery.

Example:

Date	Customer		Open Commitment
March 2	A	Bought 1 Dec Gold	
	B	Bought 2 Dec Gold	
	C	Sold 2 Dec Gold	
	D	Sold 1 Dec Gold	
		Open Commitment at end of day	3
March 3	E	Bought 1 Dec Gold	
	F	Sold 1 Dec Gold	
		Open Commitment at end of day	4
March 4	A	Sold 1 Dec Gold	(Liquidation)
	F	Bought 1 Dec Gold	
		Open Commitment at end of day	3

Note: Only one side is counted (buy *or* sell).

Also known as: *Open Interest*

Opening (Call)	A controlled method of opening a market; opening call is administered by an exchange official.
Opening Margin	See: *Initial Margin*
Opening Only	An order placed for execution at opening call of the trading session. This time limit may be given with or without a price limit.

> **Example:**
> Buy 5M July Soybeans Market Opening Only
> or
> Buy 5M July Soybeans 570 Opening Only

> The first order is to be executed during the exchange-specified opening period at the best available price. The second order is to be executed during the exchange-specified opening period at a price of 570 or better; if the price criterion is not met, the order is not executed.

Opening Price	The price at the start of a trading day.

> In a broader sense, when the market has a price range at which bids and offers are made or transactions completed during the opening period of the market. Orders may be filled anywhere within that price range.

> **Also known as:** *Opening Range*

> **See:** *Closing Price/Closing Range*
> *Clearing Price/Settlement Price*

Opening Range	See: *Opening Price*
Opening (The)	An exchange-designated period at the beginning of a trading session during which transactions are considered made "at the opening."
Open Interest	See: *Open Commitment*
Open Order	See: *Good til Cancelled/Resting Order*
Open Outcry	A public-auction method of trading in which bids and offers are audible to all participants in the trading ring.
Open Policy	See: *Floating Policy*
Open Position	See: *Open Contract*
Open Trade	A transaction not yet closed out or liquidated. This term is sometimes used interchangeably with *open contract*.
Open Trade Equity	The value remaining after calculating unrealized profits and subtracting unrealized loss on all open positions.

> **Example:**

Open Position	Trade Price	Settlement Price	Profit or Loss
Long 4 May Copper	65.00	66.00	$1,000.00 cr
Short 1 July Copper	67.20	68.50	325.00 dr
Net Copper	*(gain)*		$ 675.00
Long 2 July Cocoa	2400	2450	$1,000.00 cr
Net Cocoa	*(gain)*		$1,000.00

Note:

Profit (Loss) = (Settlement Price − Trade Price) × Factor × Quantity

In the above account,

Net Copper	675.00 profit
Net Cocoa	1,000.00 profit
	1,675.00 open trade equity

Option

A contract in which the seller gives the buyer the right to a commodity at a designated price over a stipulated time period. The seller receives compensation known as a premium for granting the contract.

Call options represent the possible ultimate purchase of the commodity. Put options represent the possible ultimate sale of the commodity.

Option (U.S. Domestic)

An exchange-traded contract to buy or sell an underlying commodity contract at a specified strike price with the buyer having the right to the futures any time up to the expiration date.

An option can be

1. *Buy a call:* An option with the right to a long futures contract on demand.
2. *Sell a Call:* An option with the obligation to go short a futures contract, if exercised.
3. *Buy a Put:* An option with the right to a short futures contract on demand.
4. *Sell a Put:* An option with the obligation to go long a futures contract, if exercised.

A U.S. commodity option may be exercised or offset by liquidation or abandonment.

Option/Futures Spreads

An option is paired, for margin purposes, with a futures position. When the option is a call, the futures is the opposite side. When the option is a put, the futures is the same side.

Example:

Option Position	*Futures Position*
Long 1 July Sugar #11 Call	Short 1 July Sugar #11
Short 1 July Sugar #11 Call	Long 1 July Sugar #11
Long 1 July Sugar #11 Put	Long 1 July Sugar #11
Short 1 July Sugar #11 Put	Short 1 July Sugar #11

Option/Option Spreads

A long option is paired, for margin purposes, with a short option of the same class (call to call, put to put).

Example:

Long 1 Dec T-bond Call @ 58
Short 1 Dec T-bond Call @ 60
Long 1 Dec T-bond Put @ 66
Short 1 Dec T-bond Put @ 68

Sometimes this spread is call a *straddle*.

See: *Dual Option*

Option Period

The period of time during which the option can be exercised or assigned.

Example:

Long 1 Feb COMEX Gold Call 400 Strike Expiration February 10

The option period runs from the time of original purchase to the expiration date of February 10. This period is part of the option contract agreement.

Option Trading

The purchasing or writing of option contracts.

Also known as: *Privilege Trading*

Order

A buy or sell instruction.

Order Desk

A fixed location (one or more desks) with communication lines to the exchange floors. The person(s) manning the order desk is responsible for placing orders with the floor broker.

Order Number

The unique designation established and assigned by an organization to identify and control orders and, ultimately, verify execution.

Order Rack

A filing system that holds orders awaiting execution in a commodity-month-time-entered sequence for ready reference.

Order Ticket

The official brokerage document that an order is written on when received from the customer.

Original Margin

See: *Initial Margin/Opening Margin/Security Deposit*

Original Margin Call

See: *Initial Margin Call*

OTC Options

A currency option written by a bank and held on its own books rather than being traded.

Out-of-the-Money

An expression of the relationship of an option to the underlying futures contract. An out-of-the-money option is one with no intrinsic value. For a call—both long and short—the strike price of the option is *higher* than the current price of the underlying futures contract. For a put—both long and short—the strike price of the option is *lower* than the underlying futures contract. This relationship may be a factor in determining margin requirements.

Example:
COMEX FEBRUARY GOLD

Futures Settlement Price 400.00

Option:

Strike Price	Market Price Call	Put
380	10.00	2.00
400	1.30	13.30
420	.20	32.20

Calls, both long and short, trading at a strike of 420 are considered out-of-the-money. Puts, both long and short, trading at a strike of 380 are considered out-of-the-money.

To determine the amount the option is out-of-the-money:

Out-of-the-Money = (Difference between the Futures Settlement and Option Strike) × Factor × Quantity

One call, either long or short, at 420 in the example would be

Out-of-the-Money $= (420 - 400) \times 100 \times 1$
Out-of-the-Money $= \$2,000.00$

One put, either long or short, at 380 in the example would be

Out-of-the-Money $= (400 - 380) \times 100 \times 1$
Out-of-the-Money $= \$2,000.00$

See: *At-the-Money*
Deep-out-of-the-Money
In-the-Money

Out Trade

A trade that does not compare in the clearing process.

Overbought

A technical opinion of the condition of the market when market prices have risen too steeply and quickly in relation to underlying fundamental factors.

See: *Oversold*

Overload(ing)

A condition in which a commodity is loaded into a rail car, truck or barge such that it exceeds the weight limit that the carrier may carry lawfully and is too full for proper inspection.

Oversold

A technical opinion of the condition of the market when market prices have declined too steeply and quickly in relation to underlying fundamental factors.

Also known as: *Sold-out Market*

See: *Overbought*

PA

The standard abbreviation for *Power of Attorney*, a written authorization in which one party enables another to act as an agent capable of making decisions.

Power of Attorney may be "limited" specifying the exact authority conveyed, such as trading only; or "general," "full" or total power conveying unrestricted power inclusive of managing cash and entering into any contract.

The document authorizing a power of attorney.

Also known as: *POA*

P&F Chart

The standard abbreviation for *Point and Figure Chart*, a chart constructed to detail a continuous flow of price activity without regard to time. Plotting direction is determined by a preset number of price changes in sequential order. See Illustration P-1.

See: *Bar Chart*
Daily High-Low Chart

P&S

The standard abbreviation for *purchase and sale (statement)*, an accounting statement advising the client of contract close-out details, including commission and fees, as well as profit or loss.

Example:
Account XYZ P&S #9999

	Bought	Sold	Commodity	Trade Price
	1		Dec COMEX Gold	400.00
		1	Dec COMEX Gold	420.00
			Gross Profit	$2,000.00
			Commission and Fees	162.50
			Net Profit	$1,837.50

```
              X
              XX
              XXX
350           00X0        Point and Figure
           X  XXXX
           X  XX X
           XX X  X
           XXXX  XX
345        5555  555  5
           XXXX  XXX  XXX
           XXX   X XX XXXX
           X        XXXXXXX        X
                    XXXXX X      X X
340                 0000  0      000
                    XXXX  X      XXX
                    XXXX  X   X  XX
                     X X  X   XXX
                          X   XXX
335                       55 555
                          XXXXXX
                          XXXXX
                          XXX
                          XX
330                       0

          Time is not Plotted Horizontally
```

Illustration P-1

Paper Profits/Losses

Seemingly earned profits (losses) calculated on current market value against original contract value of an open position(s). Paper profits are subject to change on a daily basis.

Example:
On March 2 (9:30 a.m.)

Buy 1 Dec COMEX Gold 425.00

At the close of the trading day the settlement price of December COMEX gold is 430.00.

To calculate profit or loss:

Profit (Loss) = (Settlement Price − Trade Price) × Factor × Quantity

therefore,

Paper Profit = ($430.00 − $425.00) × 100 × 1 = $500.00

If on March 3 the settlement price of December COMEX Gold is 428.00, the paper profits on the same trade change to

($428.00 − $425.00) × 100 × 1 = $300.00

Note: Actual profits (losses) can only be applied to the cash balance in the account at the time of close-out.

Also known as: *Unrealized Profit/Loss*

Note: Tax laws require federal taxation on these values at year end.

Paper Refinery

A reflection of the process of refining, which exists in "writing" only. What would be realized rather than what is actual at the given point in time is shown.

> **Example:** A crack spread reflects the cycle of oil in crude form as well as in byproduct form after processing.

Papers

Any of the various credentials or authorization documents required to trade commodities.

> **Example:**
> Customer Agreement
> Corporate Resolution
> Risk Disclosure Statement
> Power of Attorney

Documents that substantiate sale, payment, ownership, and/or movement of commerce.

Par

See: *Basis Grade*
Face Value

Paris Spread

See: *Crush (Spread)*

Parity

A government-determined price relationship between a commodity price and other prices in the economy.

Payee

The party to whom a negotiable instrument or draft is made payable.

> **Example:** On a check: Pay to the order of ABC. ABC is the payee.

See: *Drawee*
Drawer

Payment

A sum given or received in settlement of an obligation or agreement.

Pennant

On a price chart, a pattern in which price swings, moving in a narrowing range, tend to come to a point. Highs move lower and lows move higher with each swing. See Illustration P-2.

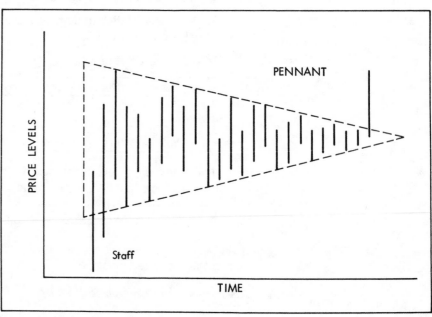

Illustration P-2

134

Also known as: *Symmetrical Triangle*

See: *Ascending Triangle*
Descending Triangle

Perishable

Goods subject to quick spoilage.

> **Example:**
> Eggs
> Potatoes
> Unprocessed fruit
> Fresh meat

Petrodollars

U.S. dollars held by oil-exporting countries.

Phantom Freight

Charges passed on to a buyer that were not actually incurred by the seller, such as shipping charges to a location farther away than the actual destination.

Physicals

See: *Actuals/Cash/Spot*

Piggybacking

A method of freight transportation in which two types of vehicles are used at once.

> **Example:** A truck trailer loaded with goods is itself transported by rail flat-car. When the shipment reaches the destination, the trailer is hitched to a tractor to continue the delivery. This method of transportation is usually cheaper than truck transport for the whole trip.

See: *Fishybacking*

Pit

An area of the exchange floor designated for executing orders for a given commodity.

Also known as: *(Trading) Ring*

> **Example:** See Illustration P-3. The pit floor (well) is reserved for exchange use. Brokers are not allowed to stand in this area. The trading steps, indicated by X's, are platform areas where the brokers stand to execute orders.

Note: Some pit rings have designated areas for a specified trading month or months. Brokers standing in these areas trade only that month or months.

Pit Trader

See: *Executing Broker*
Floor Broker

Pit Trading

See: *Auction*

Plus Tick

A price higher than the immediately preceding sale's price.

> **Example:**
> Composite Index (N.Y. Futures Exchange):

9:00 a.m.	Trade 1	68.00
	2	68.00
9:05 a.m.	Trade 3	67.90
	4	68.00

Trade 4 represents a plus tick.

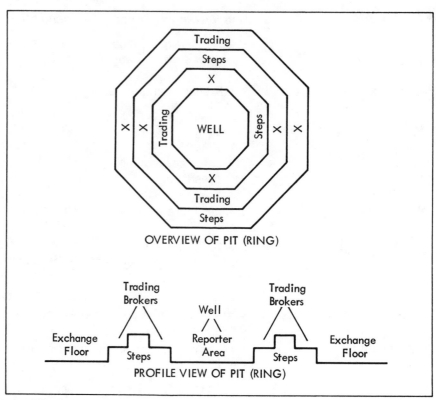

OVERVIEW OF PIT (RING)

PROFILE VIEW OF PIT (RING)

Illustration P-3

See: *Down Tick/Minus Tick*
Zero Plus Tick

Point **See:** *Basis Point*

Point and Figure Chart **See:** *P&F Chart*

Point Balance An inventory control required of every futures commission broker handling customer business. This control assures that futures positions being reported to the client as being open or committed are equal in value to a control account reflecting daily accumulated money settlements received from the clearing house. Number of contracts by commodity and trading month are also verified in the procedure.

A report that details open positions at both current settling price and original trade price and is used for position verification, liquidation applications, and reconciliations.

Point Balancing The method of reconciling open positions and monies to general and clearing house control accounts.

Example:

	Contracts	Value
Customer A	5	$4,500.00 cr
Customer B	3	2,650.00 cr
Clearing Account	8	7,150.00 cr

Point Value The dollar-and-cents value of the smallest increment price movement permitted in a price change.

Example:

	Factor Value
Wheat ¼c per bushel	$12.50
Bonds 1/32 of a dollar	31.25
Sugar 1/100¢ per lb.	11.20

Note: All future contracts do not have a minimum fluctuation equal to the smallest increment price movement, such as the meat markets that can change by 2½ points. In this instance the minimum fluctuation equals $10, but the point value equals $4.

Pool

A trust or syndicate that solicits and accepts orders for a common fund of a speculative venture.

To combine efforts or resources to satisfy a mutual need.

Port

A city, harbor, or other place used for the entrance or exit of ships.

Port of Entry

A government-designated port with facilities for clearing goods for entry into the country, such as regulatory people, customs, etc.

Position

A contract or interest in the market.

The nature of an open contract, such as long or short.

Position Limit

The maximum number of contracts that one entity can hold under the rules of the Commodity Futures Trading Commission and/or the authorized trading exchange.

Position limits are stipulated for each clearing broker by the clearing houses, according to the capital structure of the individual broker.

Position limits are stipulated by each exchange for the commodity that any one person or single entity may hold or control. The Commodity Futures Trading Commission approves the exchange ruling for maximum limits.

Note: A customer trading at more than one brokerage firm is responsible for observing maximum limits for the aggregate of his/her holdings.

Position Report

A document prepared by a clearing member that reports by trade date all open positions in a spot (delivery) month on their books.

The clearing house utilizes this information to coordinate deliveries.

Position Trading

An approach to trading in which contracts are bought or sold and retained on a long-term basis versus rapid turnover for quick profits.

See: *Day Trade*

Position Trader

A participant—speculator or hedger—who holds positions for a period of time.

See: *Day Trader*
Scalper

Possible Price

The unspecified or unknown price of one of the legs of a spread which is later set within the given daily range.

Spread trading is executed on the differential of two values. Prices are not necessarily established at the moment of execution but still must be fixed and reported to the clearing house by the end of the day. The price is set between the price limits for the given transaction day.

Example: Entered spread order:

Buy 5M May Wheat
Sell 5M July Wheat 10¢ July over May price to be fixed

Futures traded at

May 340, 345, 346, 350, 355
July 351, 355, 354, 360

Execution reported

Bought 5M May Wheat @ 351
Sold 5M July Wheat @ 361

The trader elected to establish the May price at 351. This is allowable even though 351 was not actually traded. The price to be fixed had to be anywhere between 340 and 355, the actual range for May. The July price was calculated for 10¢ over May to satisfy the order. The price of 361 was not traded and also fell outside the actual traded range. This is also acceptable, as long as the July price does not fall outside the permitted daily range.

Note: The prices reported to the exchange do not affect the actual sequence of prices established earlier.

Spread trades are published separately from regular trading.

See: *Actual Price*
Price Setting

Postdate

The dating of a document later than the actual date on which it is executed.

Example: Today's date is November 10. A check is dated December 15.

Note: The instrument is not usable until December 15.

See: *Predate*

Posted Price

An exchange recording of an official price level being established by trade.

Power of Attorney

See: *PA*

Prearranged Trade

Trading that takes place between brokers in accordance with an agreement or understanding. The competition of the auction market is avoided.

Note: This is an illegal transaction.

Predate

The dating of a document earlier than the actual date on which it is executed.

Example: Today's date is November 10. The two signing parties agree to an earlier starting or retroactive date. The contract is dated November 1.

See: *Postdate*

Preferential Tariff

A tariff favoring one or more nations over others; generally a preferential rate is a lower rate.

Premium

The amount (price) agreed upon between the purchaser and the grantor. For an exchange-traded U.S. domestic option it is:

Trade Price × Factor × Quantity = Premium

---

and is paid by the purchaser and passed through the clearing house as settlement of the agreement to the grantor.

Example:

Option	Trade Price
Bought 1 Oct Sugar #11 Call @ 18	1.75

Trade Price	× Factor ×	Quantity =	Premium
1.75	1120	1	$1,960.00

Other traded options are paid by the purchaser directly to the seller.

Also known as: *Settlement Premium*

See: *Premium Market Value*
Settlement Price (Option)

An additional payment charged for delivery of a higher standard or grade of a commodity.

Example: No. 1 Hard Red Winter Wheat is at a 1-cent premium to No. 3 Red Winter Wheat.

The excess of one price—futures to futures price or cash market price.

Example:

Mar Wheat	3.41	(Chicago)
Mar Wheat	3.77	(Kansas City)

Kansas City wheat is selling at a premium to Chicago Wheat.

When used for price relationships between different months of a commodity, the greater price is considered trading at a premium over the other(s).

Example:

Heating Oil	April	$80.30
	May	78.90

April heating oil is selling at a premium to May heating oil.

The amount paid or received for insurance coverage, protection.

Premium Market Value

The full value of an option that can be received in the market place on a given day. The formula used is

---

Option settlement price × Factor × Quantity

Example:

Option	Trade Price
Long 1 Oct Sugar #11 Call @ 18	1.75

If on a given day the settlement price for October Sugar #11 Call at 18 is $1.80, the premium market value for that contract is

Option Settlement Price	× Factor ×	Quantity =	Premium
1.80	1120	1	$2,016.00

Price	**See:** *Actual Price/Cash Price/Spot Price* *Contract Price* *Market Price* *Possible Price* *Posted Price* *Settlement Price (Option)* *Term Price* *Trade Price*
Price Basing	The practice of using the prices of futures trading to estimate cash prices in localized markets and related services such as storage, transportation, or processing.
Price Fixing	**See:** *Fixing the Price*
Price Insurance	**See:** *Hedging*
Price Limit	**See:** *Basis Point/Minimum Price Fluctuation* *Maximum Price Fluctuation*
Price Setting	The practice of determining the prices of the legs of a spread that was traded on a differential. Differential is determined by competitive bid and offer. Prices are set outside the ring.

Example:

Long 5M May Wheat
Short 5M July Wheat
10-point spread, May price to be fixed.

The 10-point spread is determined by competitive bid and offer. The actual prices are set later, outside the ring, and must be within the trading limits of the day.

See: *Actual Price*
Possible Price

Primary Market	The principal trading center for a given commodity.
Prime Rate	The lowest interest rate charged by commercial banks to their most credit worthy corporate customers. This rate is also the basis for determining interest rates on other loans granted.
Privilege Trading	**See:** *Option Trading*
Pro	The standard abbreviation for *proforma bill of lading*, an inland document used in the transport of goods via truck between port and points of origin or destination and containing marks, steamship line, etc. This document is matched to the dock receipt. **Also known as:** *Pro Ticket* If the mode of transportation is rail, the document is called a *waybill*.
Profit Taking	The closing out of positions to realize actual profits.
Proforma Bill of Lading	**See:** *Pro*
Proforma Statement	A statement that serves as a model but does not reflect reality.

For example, a proforma invoice is the original document accounting for the transaction that has taken place; but unrealized charges, costs, adjustments, etc., are not included but are adjusted via a subsequent document. A proforma invoice is used for budget purposes or to obtain necessary documents for import or export purposes.

Promissory Note

A written promise to pay a specific amount to another party or to bearer at a specified time or on demand.

Prompt Date

The specific date on which a contract must be delivered and settled. This term is used primarily for London Metals.

Proprietary Account

An account owned by a brokerage house; or one's own personal trading account, with no outside or customer interest. Proprietary accounts are not segregated when a clearing member operates his/her own trading account.

Pro Ticket

See: *Pro*

Purchase and Sale (Statement)

See: *P&S*

Purchase Price

The total actual cost paid, or to be paid, to acquire a contract.

Purchaser

See: *Buyer/Taker*

Put

An exchange-traded option contract that gives the purchaser the right, but not the obligation, to enter into an underlying futures contract to be short the commodity at a stated strike price any time prior to the expiration of the option. The grantor of the put has the obligation, upon exercise, to deliver the short futures contract.

See: *Call*

Pyramiding

See: *Averaging Up*

Qualified Endorsement

An endorsement on an instrument that has limitations in liability in the event of nonpayment.

    Example: A sales agreement is noted "Without recourse."

See: *Endorsement*

Quantity

The number of contract units agreed to in a trade. Grains are measured in thousands of bushels; other contracts are in units of one, reflecting various weights or values as determined by the respective commodity contract specifications.

The physical weight or value of one contract per the contract rules: bushels, pounds, ounces, loads, square feet, dollars, etc.

Quota

A limit upon the amount of goods that can be imported into a given country for a given period of time.

Quotation/Quote

See: *Bid and Ask*

Raid

An illegal attempt to cause prices to drop.

Rally

A rapid rise in price following a decline.

Also known as: *Recovery*

See: *Reaction*

Range

The high and low prices recorded during a specified time, such as a trading session, a week, month, or year.

The high and low bids and offers recorded during a specified time.

RCR

See: *Account Executive/AE*

Reaction

A decline in price following an advance.

See: *Rally/Recovery*

Realized Profit (Loss)

The actual profit (loss) taken on a closed-out position.

Example:

Buy	Sell	Commodity	Trade Price	
1		Dec COMEX Gold	400.00	
	1	Dec COMEX Gold	420.00	
		Gross Profit		$2,000.00
		Less *Commission/Fees*		162.50
		Net Profit		$1,837.50

The realized profit on the trade is $1,837.50

Realized profits or losses are reported to the customer on a P & S statement. The positions no longer appear in the customer's trading account. The money is automatically added to the account's ledger balance.

See: *Paper Profits (Losses)/Unrealized Profits (Losses)*

Reauthorization

An extension of lifetime or allowance to continue as an entity.

> **Example:** The Commodity Futures Trading Commission requires reauthorization from Congress to continue operation.

Reconciliation

The process of manually bringing an account to current status by noting all accounting adjustments that affect the recorded balance.

This process is executed when proving control accounts to their subsidiary accounts.

Recovery

See: *Rally*

Redeliver

The practice whereby the long futures contract holder receives delivery of the commodity and elects to reissue or resell that quantity or less within contract specifications against short futures contract(s).

Red Month(s)

Futures-contract trading month(s) that are a year distant and trade concurrently with identical near-term current trading month(s).

> **Example:** Chicago Wheat trades 18 months into the future. (For purposes of this example the current calendar month is April.) Active months for the Wheat contract are as shown in Illustration R-1.

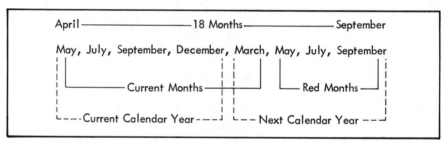

Illustration R-1

Note: Red months are a year in advance; however, current calendar year or crop year do not influence the methodology.

Reference Trade

The identification of an established open position that may be used for liquidation or some other adjusting condition.

See: *Special vs. Trade*

Registered Commodity Representative (RCR)

See: *Account Executive/AE*

Registration Fees

The cost to be registered with the Commodity Futures Trading Commission as a commission broker. The National Futures Association assumes the processing duties of registration.

Regularity

A processing plant, warehouse, or vault that satisfies exchange requirements for financing, facilities, or location for delivery of commodities against futures contracts.

Regulated Account	A general ledger or customer account that reflects the accounting of commodities traded on an authorized exchange and subject to the jurisdiction of the Commodity Futures Trading Commission.
	Proprietary accounts are the exception.
	See: *Nonregulated Account*
Regulated Commodity	A commodity traded on an authorized exchange and subject to regulation by the Commodity Futures Trading Commission.
	Also known as: *Regulated Futures Contract (RFC)*
	See: *Nonregulated/Unregulated*
Regulated Futures Contract	**See:** *Regulated Commodity*
Regulations	Rules of conduct directed, managed, or controlled by a given authority, such as the Commodity Futures Trading Commission, and applied to the exchanges and participants of the industry.
	This term is sometimes used interchangeably with *Rules*.
	See: *Rules*
Reinstate	Restoration of a previous position after a liquidation or other adjustment.
Related Accounts	Connected accounts that have the same financial interests of ownership and that are grouped together for reportable position limitations.
	Note: The account titles do not need to be the same.
	Example: Accounts with Mr. Jones as principal: Mr. Jones Mr. & Mrs. Jones Jones & Smith (joint account) ABC Corporation (Jones Pres.) Jones Investments (advisory account)
	If all these accounts are open and trading at the same time, their positions must be aggregated under the account of Mr. Jones.
Remittance	The payment of a debt or financial obligation.
Reopening	A procedure initiated after the official opening when trading has been suspended briefly in erratic markets.

Example:
Coffee Market

Market opens	9:45 a.m.	
Market is closed	10:30 a.m.	by exchange because of volume
Reopening	10:45 a.m.	directed by the exchange
Normal close	2:28 p.m.	

Note: Although it is uncommon, a market can be reopened any number of times during a trading session. Such procedures are the responsibility of exchange officials.

Report	The verbal and/or written confirmation of an executed order being received from the exchange floor.
	An account of activity, accounting and/or statistical information.

Example:
Trade Blotter
Bank Reconciliation
Customer Status
Crop Yield

Reportable

An account that accumulates in one commodity month the regulatory maximum number of positions one person is permitted to hold. At this point, a daily report of the positions must be made to an exchange and or the Commodity Futures Trading Commission.

Reportable Positions

The number of contracts specified by the Commodity Futures Trading Commission (CFTC) at which one must begin reporting total positions by delivery month to the authorized exchange and/or the CFTC.

Also known as: *Reporting Limit, Reporting Level*

Reporting Level/Limit

See: *Reportable Positions*

Requirement

See: *Margin*

Resistance Area

On a bar chart, the price level previously reached and through which the market must trade before continuing in that direction. See Illustration R-2.

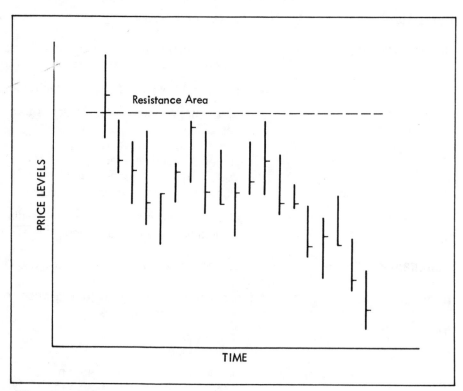

Illustration R-2

See: *Congestion Area*
 Support Area

Respondent

In the arbitration process or reparation proceeding, the party against whom a claim is made.

See: *Arbitrator*
 Claimant

Resting Order

See: *Good til Cancelled/Open Order*

| **Restriction** | An account designation signifying failure to meet margin calls properly or violation of compliance rules. |

Restriction

An account designation signifying failure to meet margin calls properly or violation of compliance rules.

Note: Only trades to liquidate already held positions are permitted when an account is under restriction.

Restrictive Endorsement

An endorsement on an instrument that indicates a transfer for a specific purpose.

Example: "For deposit only" written on a check prevents the check from being used to satisfy any other payment.

See: *Endorsement*

Retender

The right of a holder of a long futures contract who has been tendered a delivery notice to resell the obligation via an offering in the futures market. This practice is permissible only if trading after notice of intention is received is permitted by the given contract market.

This trade, once executed, is unique in that it cannot be used to liquidate any long open position, nor can it be liquidated by a subsequent purchase. Once committed, the seller must tender a notice of delivery intention.

See: *Tender*

Such a position (trade).

Revenue

The total amount obtained from a sale.

Reversal Chart

A type of chart in which a price trend must be reversed by a predetermined amount before being posted to the chart. This chart is used as a control device to assure a true price movement rather than a chance spontaneous fluctuation. See Illustration R-3.

```
                          X   X              X
                          X   XX             X
                          X   XX             XX  X
              840         0    00            00000
                          XX  X              XXXXX
                          XXXX               XXXXX
                          XXXX               XXXXX
                          X  XX              X  X  X
              835          55                       5 5
                           XX                        XX
                           X                         XX
                                                     XX
                                                     XX
              830                                    0


                          Three              Five
                          Point              Point

                          REVERSAL PATTERNS
```

Illustration R-3

Reversal Pattern

A price pattern on a bar chart indicating a trend change. Examples include head and shoulders, descending triangle, or a "W" (double bottom) formation. See Illustration R-4.

See: *Consolidation Pattern/Continuation Pattern*

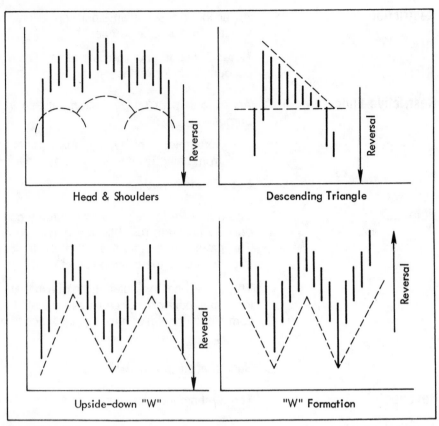

Head & Shoulders   Descending Triangle

Upside-down "W"   "W" Formation

Illustration R-4

Reverse Conversion

Three positions, combined for margin purposes, consisting of a long call, a short put, and a short futures. The expiration month must be the same for all three positions and the strike price the same for the two option positions.

Example:

Option	Strike Price
Long 1 Dec T-bond	Call @ 60
Short 1 Dec T-bond	Put @ 60

Futures	Trade Price
Short 1 Dec T-bond	@ 64 8/32

See: *Conversion*

Reverse Crush Spread

A spread between soybeans and soybean byproducts in which soybean futures are sold and soybean oil and meal are purchased.

Example:

Short 5M bushels Sept Soybeans
Long 1 contract Sept Soybean Oil
Long 1 contract Sept Soybean Meal

Also known as: *Source Product Spread*

See: *Commodity Product Spread*
Crush Spread

Revocable

Something that can be rescinded or cancelled at will or under given conditions.

See: *Irrevocable*

RFCs	**See:** *Regulated Commodities*
Ring	**See:** *Pit*
Risk	The extent of potential loss.
Risk Disclosure Statement	A written statement informing customers of risks and responsibilities in commodity trading, such as margin procedures and practices and limitations of trade activities in the market. This document helps a customer determine his/her own suitability for trading in the market and must be signed before any trading can take place.
Rolling Forward	The moving of a position held in one trading month of a commodity by trading out of it and reestablishing that same position in a later month of that commodity on the same exchange.

Example:

Open Position for Account XYZ

Long 2 Apr Hogs

A trade comes in for the account to sell 2 April Hogs, which liquidates the open long position.

A second trade comes in for the account to buy 2 June Hogs, which establishes a new long position in June replacing the liquidated April position.

A trading procedure involving the liquidation of a straddle position in a given delivery month of a commodity and the simultaneous initiation of a similar position in another month of the same commodity on the same exchange while holding the untraded position of the straddle. The straddle is shifted by combining the new position with the untraded leg of the original straddle, creating a new straddle.

Example:

Open Position for Customer XYZ

Long 2 Apr Hogs straddled with
Short 2 June Hogs

The following trades were executed:

Sold 2 April Hogs (for liquidation against long open position)
Bought 2 July Hogs (new position to be straddled with the open June position)

Open Position After Trading

Long 2 July Hogs straddled with
Short 2 June Hogs

Also known as: *Rollover/Switch(ing)*

See: *Swap(ping)*

Rollover	**See:** *Rolling Forward*
Round Lot	A full contract or standard quantity of a commodity equal in size to the futures contract of that commodity.

Example:

Platinum	50 troy ounces
Wheat	5,000 bushels

See: *Job Lot/Odd Lot*

Round(ing) Bottom

On a chart, a reversal price pattern consisting of minor price swings in a slow-moving market in which a downward trend gradually reverses upward. See Illustration R-5.

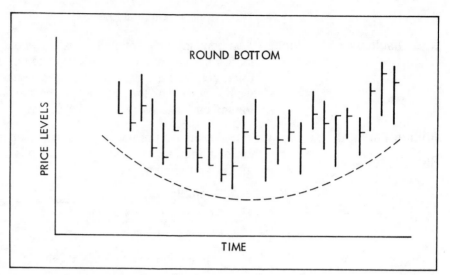

Illustration R-5

Also known as: *Saucer Bottom, Scallop Bottom*

See: *Round(ing) Top/Saucer Top/Scallop Top*

Round(ing) Top

On a chart, a reversal price pattern consisting of minor price swings in a slow-moving market in which an upward trend gradually reverses downward. See Illustration R-6.

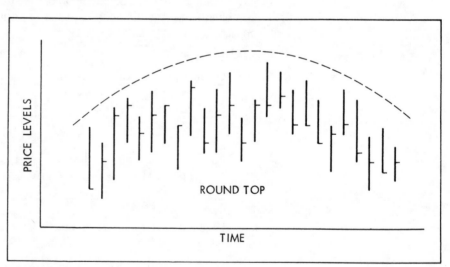

Illustration R-6

Also known as: *Saucer Top, Scallop Top*

See: *Rounding Bottom/Saucer Bottom/Scallop Bottom*

Roundturn

The combination of an initiating purchase or sale of a futures contract(s) and the offsetting sale or purchase of the same quantity and delivery month for commission purposes.

See: *Close-out*

A method of calculating commission at completion of close-out (buy and sell combined).

Example:

Buy 1 Feb Hog (Commission)	$20.00
Sell 1 Feb Hog (Commission)	20.00
Liquidation (roundturn) Charge	$40.00

Note: The general practice of the industry is not to charge the customer on half of the trade until the liquidating side is completed. The liquidating side can be a trade or delivery or a request by the customer to transfer the trade to another broker.

See: *Halfturn*

RR

See: *Account Executive/AE/Registered Commodity Representative*

Rules

Principles, guidelines, methods, or regulations established by the board of governors of an exchange upon recommendations of various committees and based on industry trends and contract uniqueness. Rules regulate the activities of members and nonmembers in a given market.

This term is sometimes used interchangeably with *regulations.*

See: *Regulations*

Runaway Gap

On a price chart, a significant break reflecting untraded price levels between trading periods occurring during a rapidly moving market. See Illustration R-7.

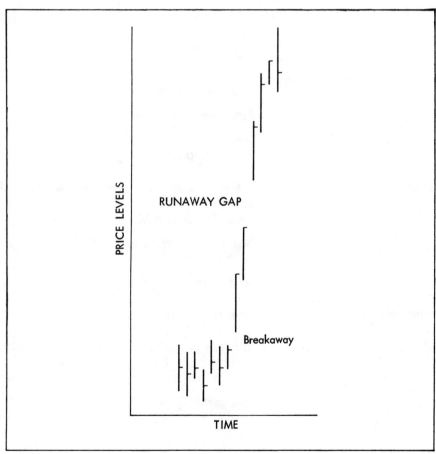

Illustration R-7

See: *Breakaway Gap*
Common Gap
Exhaustion Gap
Gap

Sale

A contract passing title (of goods) or undertaking an obligation to deliver.

Also known as: *Sell, Short*

See: *Buy/Long*
Selling Short

Sample

A small quantity of a product or a specific lot (unit) of a commodity given either to induce prospective buyers or to determine grade specifications by inspection or analysis.

Note: If sampling is specifically requested by a buyer, a fee may be charged by the seller.

Also known as: *Trier*

Sample Grade

See: *Basis Grade*

Sampling

The testing of a portion of a shipment for compliance to exchange standards. Sampling can be by visual inspection, chemical testing, or actual tasting, such as with coffee; the techniques are broad, depending on the commodity.

Evaluation by measurement of certain characteristics or events (chosen at random or by other criteria), comparisons, or known values of similar conditions.

Examples:
Beginning with January, what is the basis on the 20th of every other month?

The selection of every tenth telephone number to determine if the person prefers a given product over another given product.

Satisfaction	The fulfillment of a contract.
Saucer Bottom	**See:** *Round(ing) Bottom/Scallop Bottom*
Saucer Top	**See:** *Round(ing) Top/Scallop Top*
Scale Order	An order to buy or sell a commodity that specifies the total amount bought or sold at specified price variations.

Example:

Buy 2 Oct Cotton Market and
    2 each 10 points down total 20

may also be written as

B 2 V CTN MKT and 2 ea. 10 pts down total 20

For this order, an initial two contracts are purchased. As the day progresses, additional contracts in two's are purchased at each 10-point decline.

Initial purchase	6700
Next two due	6690
Next two	6680 etc.

Up to 20 contracts in all may be purchased. However, if the market does not have sufficient range (that is, to decline at least to 6610), the complete order cannot be filled.

Note: A market that trades at the price limit of an order does not guarantee a fill.

Sometimes used when placing a series of orders to buy or sell at specific amounts and price levels rather than one order or at market.

Example:

Sell 3 May Cocoa @ 6230 and
    3 May Cocoa @ 6235 and
    6 May Cocoa @ 6240 and
    6 May Cocoa @ 6245

Note: Although this is one order, the floor may break the order up into four parts for control purposes and handle it as limit orders.

Scallop Bottom	**See:** *Round(ing) Bottom/Saucer Bottom*
Scallop Top	**See:** *Round(ing) Top/Saucer Top*
Scalp	The initiation and liquidation of positions quickly during the same trading session for small gains.

Example: One trader

9:10 a.m. Bought 2 Oct Cotton @ 8100
9:14 a.m. Sold   2 Oct Cotton @ 8105

then

10:05 a.m. Sold   2 Oct Cotton @ 8103
10:06 a.m. Bought 2 Oct Cotton @ 8102

Note: This trader will participate during the complete trading session in this manner. The months traded, quantity, and frequency of trading are the option of the trader.

Scalper

An active trader who attempts to profit on small price changes by buying and selling on very short term (current trading day).

A floor trader who trades only his/her own account and creates liquidity by buying and selling continuously.

Also known as: *Local*

Seasonal

Affected by or occurring during a particular period of the calendar year. This factor determines a repeatable pattern influencing supplies and prices.

Example: Price Behavior:

		Price
Commodity	High	Low
Wheat	December May	August through September
Cotton	July	November through December

Seat

Membership on an organized exchange.

SEC

The standard abbreviation for the *Securities & Exchange Commission*, the federal agency with authority to regulate security trading firms and securities traded on stock exchanges. Firms that handle commodities exclusively are not subject to SEC authority.

See: *CFTC/Commodity Futures Trading Commission*

Secured Loan

A loan backed by collateral capable of being liquidated in satisfaction of a default.

Securities

Various classes of stocks, bonds, financial instruments, or other negotiable documents (assets other than cash) owned by the customer that are eligible for and presented to the broker for margin purposes.

Note: The broker reserves the right to refuse any or all such instruments for margin.

Securities on Deposit

Negotiable documents (financial instruments) deposited by a client in lieu of cash to satisfy initial margin requirements.

Also known as: *SOD*

Example:
T-bills (U.S. government obligations)
Exchange-traded stock certificates

Note: The nature and marginable value of securities are primarily determined by the various exchange margin rules. Brokers and clearing houses also have individual restrictions.

Security Deposit

See: *Initial Margin/Original Margin*

Segregated Fund

A special account used to hold and separate customers' assets from those of the broker or firm.

Bank account(s), carrying broker account(s) or any other type of account in which customer funds are being held must carry within the account title a clear indication of its purpose.

Example:

Bank	ABC Brokerage Services, Inc.
	Customer Segregated Funds
Carrying Broker	ABC Brokerage Services, Inc.
	Omnibus Account
	Customer Segregated Funds

Segregation

The recording and accounting of customers' money and securities as a separate liability distinct from the liabilities and assets of the receiving broker. Specially designated bank accounts are set up for these funds.

A government regulation requiring a broker holding customer assets, cash, equity, and securities of deposit to deposit and account for these funds separately and independently from the funds and assets of the broker.

Segregation safeguards against customer funds being utilized by the broker for private investment or being offered as payment to the broker's creditors.

Segregation Report

A daily reconciliation of segregated funds being held for customers by the broker. This document must be retained for the records of the firm and must be available for inspection by the various exchanges, the National Futures Association (NFA), or the Commodity Futures Trading Commission (CFTC).

Example:

Segregation Report

Customer Assets
  Customer Cash
  Profit and Loss on Open Trades
  Customers in Deficit
  Customer Securities on Deposit

Total Funds to be Segregated

Assets Held by Broker
  Segregated Bank Accounts (Cash)
  Margin at the Clearing Houses
  Cash with Carrying Broker
  Customer's securities in Safekeeping

Total Funds in Segregation

Assets being held by the broker must equal or be greater than the customer assets. If the reconciliation shows customer assets greater, then the firm is undersegregated and must report the condition to the Commodity Futures Trading Commission immediately.

Note: The categories of segregation used in the example are general and do not reflect a complete report. Refer to the Commodity Exchange Act regulations for a thorough description.

Sell

See: *Sale*

Seller

See: *Grantor/Writer*

Seller's Call

The sale of a specific number of futures contracts of a given commodity at a certain number of points above or below the specified delivery month with the seller given a certain period of time within which to fix the price.

Example: On August 31 the following agreement:

Sell 5M Wheat 10¢ under Dec within 1 month

Prices during the month of September are:

September 1 Dec Wheat 4.75
September 15 Dec Wheat 4.73
September 30 Dec Wheat 4.80

On September 30 the market has reacted as expected, and the seller fixes the price at 4.70 or 10 points under the market of 4.80.

See: *On Call*
Buyer's Call

Seller's Market

A high-demand, short-supply market in which sellers command higher-than-normal prices or better conditions.

See: *Buyer's Market*

Selling Hedge

The sale of a contract to protect against decreases in prices of commodities to be sold in the future.

Example: A farmer growing 20,000 bushels of wheat in March estimates that the wheat must be sold for at least $3.75 per bushel. The July futures contract is selling at $3.91 per bushel. If the difference between the July futures price and the anticipated cash selling price is equal to or greater than the normal basis, the farmer will hedge (sell) the equivalent numbers of contracts.

March 15

Cash
Estimated yield 20,000 bushels of Wheat Price objective is $3.75 per bushel

Futures
Sells 4 contracts July Wheat @ $3.91 per bushel

In July the farmer will face one of the following situations:

Prices decline		
Cash Wheat is selling at		$3.70
Futures (July) original sale Bought (liquidation)	$3.91 3.86	
Futures profit		.05
Price received by farmer		$3.75

Prices advance		
Cash Wheat is selling at		$3.80
Futures (July original sale) Bought (liquidation)	$3.91 3.96	
Futures loss		.05
Price received by farmer		$3.75

Note: The example does not reflect money costs or commission charges.

Selling Short

A method of trading in which an individual sells a contract of a given commodity and buys at a later time to cover the sale, creating an offset and fulfilling the obligation to deliver.

Establishing a short futures contract.

Note: The customer may own the physical commodity and establish a short contract for his/her protection. The futures is still considered selling short as he/she may trade out rather than choosing to deliver the physical.

Selling the Bulge

A trading strategy that aims at obtaining the best possible selling price in a downward-moving market on the intermediate rallies (bulges).

Intermediate rallies (bulges) may occur within one trading session or may extend over several days. See Illustration S-1.

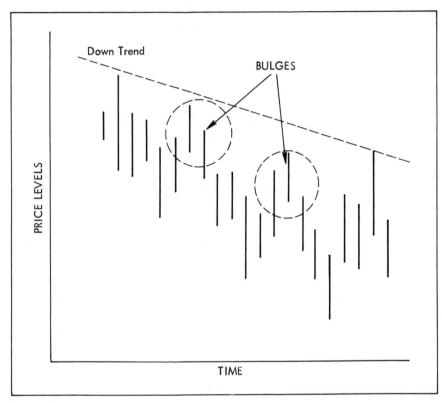

Illustration S-1

Selling the Weakness

The practice among technicians of selling markets that show downward direction. Technical happenings will inspire the trader to sell initial or additional commitments.

This term is also used when willing sellers are satisfied, leaving a vacuum effect in the market, thereby allowing few buyers to cause a rally in prices. This weak buying vanishes with renewed selling. Consequently, new sellers are selling the weakness.

See: *Weak Hands*

Sell on Close

An instruction to sell a contract during the end of the day's trading at the best possible price (at or near closing price), unless a specified price limit is given.

Example:

Sell 5,000 Sept Soybeans on the close

may also be written as

S 5M U BNS OC

Execution will take place sometime during the exchange-specified closing period (between the warning bell that signals entering the close and the final closing bell) of the market. Price is not guaranteed, except that it must be within the range of prices for the closing period.

Note: If the order has a price limit, then the execution must be at that price or higher while still within the closing range.

See: *Buy on Close*

Sell on Open

An instruction to sell a contract during the beginning of the day's trading at the best possible price (at or near opening price), unless a specified price limit is given.

Example:

Sell 1 Oct Soybean Oil on the open

may also be written as

S 1 V SBO Opening Only

This order can be executed only during the exchange-specified opening period. Any price within the trading range is acceptable. The best price of the range or the first price posted cannot be guaranteed.

Note: If the order has a price limit, then the execution must be at that price or higher while still within the opening range.

See: *Buy on Open*

Sell or (when) Tender(ed) or to Redeliver

An order placed by the holder of a long position in the delivery period in which the order is to be executed upon notice of delivery. This action can happen only in commodities that permit trading to continue during the delivery period.

Example: A holder of a spot-month commodity gives the following order to the broker:

"When tendered" Sell 5M May Wheat at the market for retender.

Note: This order is generally given to the account executive rather than the floor broker. The floor broker ultimately receives the order

Sell 5M May Wheat at the market for retender

Sell Out

To sell all inventory being held without intentions to replace immediately.

The liquidation of holdings by an agent (broker) when a customer cannot meet margin requirements.

Series

Options of the same class (call or put) that have the same strike price and expiration.

Example: For July Sugar #11, call expiration June 15:

Option	Strike	Trade Price
July Sugar #11 Call	@ 20	3.05
July Sugar #11 Call	@ 20	3.06
July Sugar #11 Call	@ 20	3.07

Note: For a customer, trade dates and trade prices create series. For a broker, different customers, trade dates, and trade prices create series.

Services

Organizations that offer chart or trading advice.

Publications reviewing and/or summarizing current happenings of markets. Reports or letters usually require subscription fees.

Note: The U.S. government offers extensive information on domestic and foreign markets free.

Conveniences offered by brokers.

> **Example:**
> Order handling and execution
> Accounting statements
> Market information
> Trading advice

Settlement

The daily accounting and transferring of monies between the clearing members. Each daily trade transaction and open position held by the brokers is marked to the market at the close of the day. A common denominator, the settlement price, is used to arrive at all settlement monies.

> **Example:**

Today's Trade	Bought	1	@ 2700
Settlement Price Today			2750
	Collect		50
Prior Position	Long	1	
Settlement Price Yesterday			2700
Settlement Price Today			2750
	Collect		50

An agreement between parties as to terms and conditions.

Settlement Premium

See: *Premium*

Settlement Price (Futures)

The official price, established by the exchange at the close of each trading day, used as the common denominator for the given day's market settlement of variation money and the next day's price limits. Futures settlement price is used to set option strike prices and determine in-the-money and out-of-the-money conditions.

Also known as: *Settling Price*

> **Example:**

	High	Low	Closing Range	Settlement Price
Daily Range	8705	8640	8660-66	8665

Note: The settlement price is generally established at a value within the closing range. It does not necessarily equal the last price traded. If no trades occur in a contract month, the exchange creates a nominal price off the existing bid or offer or the carrying charges between contract months.

See: *Trade Price*

Settlement Price (Option)

The official price, established by the exchange at the close of each trading day, used as the common denominator in determining the value of the option.

Also known as: *Settling Price*

See: *Trade Price*

Seven Sisters	The major international oil companies.
	Examples: British Petroleum Exxon Chevron Oil Gulf Oil Mobil Oil Texaco Shell Oil
Shipment	Goods consigned to a carrier for transporting and delivery.
Shipper	A party who transports and delivers a shipment and has control over the goods.
Shipping Certificate	A receipt and part of the delivery mechanism that allows loading a product into a vessel within a specified period of time, thereby reducing the necessity of storing in a warehouse. The shipping certificate acts like the warehouse receipt in relation to delivery specifications of a permitting exchange.
Short	**See:** *Sale* A net position of excess sales. **See:** *Long*
Short Cover	**See:** *Cover*
Short Hedge	**See:** *Selling Hedge*
Short Leverage	A transaction in which a customer contracts to sell metal to a leverage firm at a given price in hopes that prices will fall and the contract can be closed out at a profit. **See:** *Long Leverage*
Short Squeeze	A condition in which short supply of a commodity forces short position holders to cover with a purchase at a higher price than the original sale, thereby taking a loss. When a short is forced to repurchase due to an inability to deliver. **Also known as:** *Squeeze*
Sight Bill/Draft	A negotiable instrument that is payable on presentation. Title remains with the seller until the draft is paid.
Silver Standard	A monetary system in which silver provides the basic value for national currency. **See:** *Gold Standard*
SOD	**See:** *Securities on Deposit*
Soft Commodity	Products that are yielding or pliable in nature. **Example:** Sugar Rubber

The term is used in distinguishing agricultural commodities from the metals in London.

See: *Hard Commodities*

Soft Currency

A national currency that is diminishing in value relative to another, more stable currency.

A situation where interest rates are low and loans are easy to arrange.

Paper rather than metallic money.

Also known as: *Soft Money*

See: *Hard Currency/Hard Money*

Soft Market

A declining market with short-term price tendencies.

Soft Money

See: *Soft Currency*

Soil Bank

A program that retires productive crop acreage to reserves or pasture land. The basic intent is to adjust for abundant crop surpluses.

> **Example:** Under the U.S. government Soil Bank Act of 1956, farmers were paid to retire crop acreage on surplus commodities by leaving the acreage idle or planting grass or trees.

Note: The Act of 1956 was deemed ineffective shortly after its adoption.

Solicitor

A person seeking business from the public in return for compensation. To actively offer U.S. commodity trading or leverage products this person must be registered with the Commodity Futures Trading Commission. The National Futures Association assumes the duties of registration.

> **Example:** The person handling customers' accounts at a brokerage firm.

Solvency

The ability to pay debts.

Source Product Spread

See: *Crush Spread*
Reverse Crush Spread

Special Customs Invoice

An official import document used to establish the value of a shipment that exceeds a specified dollar value when duty is based on value.

Special Endorsement

A signed instrument that designates a subsequent payee to whom the instrument is payable.

> **Example:** A check is made payable to ABC. ABC wishes to use that check in payment to XYZ so adds the endorsement on the reverse side of the instrument:
>
> ---
> Pay to the order of XYZ
> ---

See: *Endorsement*

Specialist

A market principal obliged to trade (for his/her own account) when public offerings are inadequate to maintain an orderly market. The specialist provides liquidity and protects customers.

Sometimes the specialist may act as a broker's broker, executing orders left in his/her trust.

Note: Commodity futures markets do not have specialists.

See: *Floor Trader/Market Maker*

Special Risk Policy

An insurance contract that covers a single cargo. Rates are negotiated for each shipment.

See: *Blanket Policy*
Floating Policy/Open Policy

Special vs. (Trade)

A specific instruction as to the exact open position to be closed out. The trade carries reference information designating the offset trade such as the date, quantity, buy/sell, price, commodity, month, and, if in an automated system, reference I.D.

Also known as: *Vs. (Trade)*

Example: A customer holds the following positions:

Date	Quantity	Commodity	Trade Price
May 10	Long 2	Mar Cocoa	@ 2300
May 12	Long 1	Mar Cocoa	@ 2310*
June 10	Long 2	Mar Cocoa	@ 2290*

*Trades liquidated in special vs.

Trade executed selling 2 March Cocoa at 2300 special versus May 12 one long at 2310 and June 10 one long at 2290.

Specifications

Detailed, written descriptions; standards.

Specific Tariff

An import duty based on a stated amount per unit rather than a percentage.

Speculate

Buying or selling involving risk for the purpose of gaining large profits rather than financial protection (hedge) or investment.

Example:
Trading Index futures with no securities portfolio
A carpenter trading grains
A bank trading cocoa

See: *Hedge*

Speculative Limits

The maximum number of futures or options contracts, not designated as hedged, that a trader can control in compliance with the given contract market.

Example:

	Spot Month	Any One Month	Months Combined
Live Hogs	300	450	1500*
Soybean Oil	540	540	540*

*All months.

Note: Individual contract months have their own limits, with the maximum an aggregated sum.

Speculator

One who supplies risk capital with the object of obtaining profits through price movements rather than for hedging (protection).

See: *Hedger*

Split Close

The inability of a market to arrive at a final price at the close.

Example:

On the closing bell of a volatile market trades occur at 340 and 341.

The close would be declared as 340–341 or 341–340 (split close).

The splitting and sequence of prices, 340–341 or 341–340 are recorded by the judgment of an exchange official.

Note: Various factors prevent officials from feeling confident in choosing one price.

A split close is not to be confused with the closing range.

See: *Closing Range*

Split Price

The quoting of more than one price on an opening or closing trade.

Example:
March Soybeans 340½–340¼

The changing with a changer mini contracts for a position in a similar market.

Example:
Mid-America Hog Contract (15,000-lb contract)
Broker Long 1 Apr Hog @ 52.50 Long 1 Apr Hog @ 52.55
Change for
Chicago Mercantile Exchange (30,000-lb contract)
Long 1 Apr Hog @ 52.52

Spoilage

Losses caused by the spoiling of goods by mildew, insects, etc., in warehouses; rotting of goods in transit; or errors in product processing.

Spot

Available at once, now for immediate delivery, and/or for immediate payment.

Spot Commodity

See: *Actuals/Cash Commodity*

Spot Margin Rate

An assessment, added to the original margin requirement, issued to the holder of any open contract, long or short, in the spot month.

Example:

Frozen Orange Juice	Spot Month
Original Margin Spot Add-on	$1,500.00 500.00
Total Requirement	$2,000.00

Spot Market

See: *Cash Market*

Spot Month

The near month or current month in which futures trading is still possible and notices can be issued to the long position holder advising that delivery is about to be made. Depending on the commodity, delivery may be the physical commodity or cash settlement in lieu of the commodity.

Example: On the *Chicago Board of Trade* for October Silver:

Last Trading Day	The fourth last business day of the month
First Notice Day	Last business day of month preceding the delivery month.
Last Notice Day	The next-to-last business day in the delivery month

Spot October is from the last business day in September through (including) the fourth last business day of October. Delivery is only during the month of October; however, the first issuance notice may be sent on the last business day of September.

See: *Back Month*

Spot Price

See: *Cash Price*

Spread(ing)

The simultaneous buying of one futures contract and selling of another futures contract in the expectation that the relationship will change so as to yield a profit upon subsequent offsetting.

The buy and sell positions in the combinations.

The term is generally accepted as synonymous with *Straddle*. See the shades of differentiations sometimes used below:

It is also said that "spread" is a Chicago term and "straddle" is of New York origin.

The term *spread* is more commonly used in grains, *straddle* for other commodities.

Example:

Long 5M July Soybeans spread with
Short 5M Sept Soybeans

Long 1 May Copper straddle with
Short 1 Dec Copper

The term *spread* has been interpreted to mean the same commodity for different months, *straddle* to mean different but related commodities with same or different months.

Example:

Long 5M July Wheat (Chicago) straddle with
Short 5M July Wheat (Kansas City)

Long 5M May Corn   (Chicago) straddle with
Short 5M May Oats   (Chicago)

Straddle has been used interchangeably with *dual option spread*, a put and call of same commodity, same exercise, and same maturity. *Spread* may be long and short in the same class—long and short puts or long and short calls.

Example:

Short 1 July Sugar #11 Call @ 20 straddle with
Short 1 July Sugar #11 Put @ 20 (dual option spread)

Note: The dual option spread is two short sales contrary to all other spread or straddle arrangements.

Example:

Long 1 Dec T-bond Call @ 68 spread with
Short 1 Dec T-bond Call @ 60

See: *Strangle*

The London International Finance Futures Exchange generally refers to *straddle* as a specific type of spread involving the same type of interest-rate or currency futures with different delivery months.

Example:

Long 1 Sept Swiss francs
Short 1 Dec Swiss francs

Spreader

A trader who uses the method of spreading.

Spread or Straddle Order

An order for both the purchase and sale of different trading months in the same commodity or different commodities and/or exchanges in which a price difference between the two contracts is given (rather than absolute values) and both are to be executed and are linked or kept together to form the spread.

Example:

Buy 5M July Soybeans and
Sell 5M May Soybeans
                    July 3¢ over May

may also be written as

B 5M N BNS S 5M K BNS SPRD
                    N 3¢ over

Squeeze

See: *Short Squeeze*

Standardization

The uniformity of terms and contract specifications of the futures markets to effectively interface with the cash (spot) markets enabling the transfer of economic risk and recording control (clearance).

Standby Letter of Credit

A document of credit issued by a third party that guarantees payment on a call basis for use anytime.

Sterling Area

Nations using the British pound as the main reserve currency (current or former Commonwealth members).

Stipulation of Compliance

In the commodity industry, the documentary assurance by an individual or firm that an administrative request or directive from the Commodity Futures Trading Commission or other regulatory body will be adhered to.

Stockpile Commodities

Commodities that the government deems essential in maintaining the economic and social welfare of the country during natural disasters and war.

Examples:
Metals (copper, silver)
Foods (grains)
Seed oils
Oil (energy)

See: *Basic Commodities*
Vital Commodities

Stop Loss Order

A contingency order instructing that a position be liquidated when the market reaches a specified price. This order initiates a new trade to liquidate an open position. This order is used to limit losses or protect profits. A stop loss order is sometimes combined with a price limit.

Example: A customer has acquired

Long 1 Dec Copper 83.30

The customer believes that if the market declines to 82.20, the purchase should be liquidated. An order is entered:

Sell 1 Dec Copper 82.20 Stop

This order may also be written as

S 1 Z COP @ 8220 X

If the December contract trades at 82.20, the order becomes a market order. The customer, however, is not guaranteed a price of 82.20.

In order to limit price risk when using a stop order, traders at times prefer to add a price limit to the order.

Example: An order is entered:

Sell 1 Dec Copper 82.20 STOP 82.00 Limit

may also be written as

S 1 Z COP 8220 X 8200 LT

If the December contract trades at 82.20, the order becomes a market order. However, the broker is limited not to sell below the 82.00 price.

Note: Placing a limit on a stop order may prevent execution and nullify the protection being sought.

Stop buy orders are placed at a price above the current market. Stop sell orders are placed at a price below the current market. See Illustration S-3.

Illustration S-3

Note: There are two views on what initiates a stop order.

1. The stop price of the order is traded in the market, or higher on a buy, lower on a sell.

2. The market is bid at the price of the buy stop or offered at the price of the sell stop without an actual trade.

The executing broker should inform the customer which of these interpretations he/she uses when the customer places a stop loss order.

See: *OB/Or Better Order*

Stopped

The final acceptance of a delivery notice by the holder of a long position.

Note: This acceptance is used in markets where delivery notices can be sold during the trading session and passed on to the new buyer. The buyer accepts delivery and informs the clearing house of the action.

Stop Price

The specific point (level) at which a stop loss order becomes a market order.

Example: In the example at Stop Loss Order, the stop price is 82.20.

Straddle

See: *Spread*

Straight Bill of Lading

A nonnegotiable bill of lading that designates the specific receiver of the shipment.

Straight Limit Order

See: *Day Order*

Straight Loan

A loan based only on the borrower's ability to pay rather than on collateral.

Straight Paper

A note, acceptance, or bill of exchange secured only on the issuer's promise to pay.

Straight Transfer

A method of moving a commodity such as grain in which the grain does not lose its identity. The transfer must be made with no intermittent stops. For example, the grain is moved from car to car with no intervening house bin.

Strangle

An option position made up of a put and a call of the same commodity and maturity but different exercise prices. The positions, when established, resemble a double option. They are usually executed in the near-term months.

Traders use this approach in an uncertain market. Generally, out-of-the-money puts and calls are traded since these options have little intrinsic value and are relatively inexpensive.

Example: The U.S. Treasury Bond market is trading at 62 with the expectation of news. The trader

Buys a 56 put @ 2/64
Buys a 68 Call @ 3/64

The strategy is that the trader profits no matter which way the market moves. If the market moves up, the call will appreciate in value. If the market moves down, the put will appreciate in value.

Note: As the futures price approaches the option strike price, that option will gain more value than the option losing value as it moves further out-of-the-money.

See: *Straddle.*

Strap	A currency option spread made of two calls and one put of the same currency.
	See: *Strip*

Strike Price	**See:** *Exercise Price/Striking Price*

Strike Price Increments

Exchange-specified intervals between option exercise/strike prices.

The increment of value between strike prices varies with each option market.

Example:

COMEX Gold 20-point intervals	CBT T-bonds 128/64th intervals
360	58 00/64
380	60 00/64
400	62 00/64
420	64 00/64

Strip

A currency option spread made up of two puts and one call of the same currency.

A series of Treasury bills maturing over a period of time.

Example: *March, June, September, December* is a one-year strip.

See: *Strap*

Stripper Wells

Oil wells producing less than a given standard quantity of barrels of oil per day.

Strong Basis	**See:** *Narrow Basis*

Subindex (Option)

The right to buy or sell a call or a put on a group of stocks that reflect a particular segment of the market at a fixed (average) price for a given period of time. Option price is based on the profit potential and the odds of achieving it by the time the contract ends.

Example:
Computer and business equipment
International oils

See: *Index (Option)*

Subsidy

Financial aid given by the government, considered to be in the public interest, aimed at stabilizing prices, and permitting an enterprise or program to continue at an unprofitable level.

Summer Crack Spread

A seasonal spread in the energy market in which gasoline is the product spread with the crude oil.

Example:

Buy 1 June Crude Oil
Sell 1 June Gasoline

See: *Crack Spread*
Winter Spread

Supply

Goods or services available for sale.

See: *Demand*

Supply Elasticity

The fluctuation of production (supplies) in relation to cash price movement. A commodity is viewed as having an elastic supply when a change in price creates a change in production.

Support Area

On a chart, a price level that was reached more than once and received adequate buying for the market to advance from that level. When markets react during advances, support areas are looked upon as rallying points. See Illustration S-4.

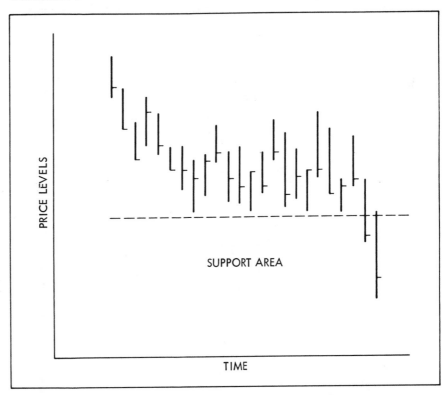

Illustration S-4

Note: The form is similar to a double bottom formation but is not looked upon as an indicator of a trend change.

See: *Congestion Area*
Resistance Area

Supported Price

A price level guaranteed by the government that prevents free market prices from declining below that point.

Surcharge

A levy on an existing tax, fee, or commission.

Example:	
Normal Commission Charge	$50.00
Cable Costs (surcharge)	3.00
Total Charge	$53.00

Surplus

Net assets over liabilities or net pluses over minuses determining the supply and demand of a given commodity.

Swap(ping)

The exchange of one position for another in a different contract month of the same commodity. This procedure is generally executed to improve financial and/or time positioning.

Example: A customer has a hedged short position at a 30-point basis. The next trading month widens its basis to 45 points, providing a 10-point premium after carrying charges.

The hedger might consider buying the currently held short futures and selling the next trading month at 15 points over.

If executed, the buy liquidates the original short position. The sale reestablishes the hedge at a better basis. (The additional length of time may or may not be relevant to the hedger.)

See: *Rollover*
Switch

Swing

A financial or economic fluctuation, activity, or movement. See Illustration S-5.

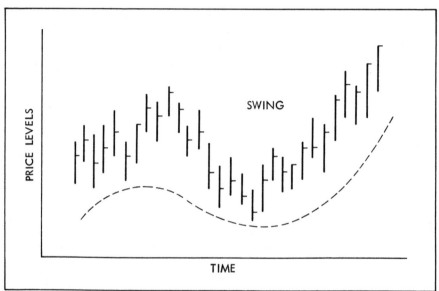

SWING

Illustration S-5

Switch(ing)

See: *Rolling Forward*
Rollover

Symmetrical Triangle

See: *Pennant*

Synthetic Option

A combination of positions that simulate or act like another position.

Example: A long futures or forward position is equivalent to buying a call and selling a put (both at the same exercise and expiration).

A short futures or forward is equivalent to buying a put and selling a call.

Loss or gain on option combinations "act like" the futures or forward equivalent.

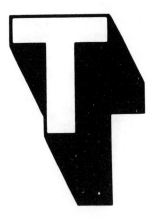

Taker
    See: *Buyer/Purchaser*

Tare
    The weight of anything used to ship materials (packing materials and vehicles).

    Note: Net weight = gross weight − tare weight.

Tariff
    See: *Duty*

Technical Analysis
    A type of market analysis that examines patterns of price changes, rates of change, and trading and open-interest volume changes to predict trends and prices. This method often employs the use of charting and/or the use of a computer.

    See: *Cyclic Analysis*
              Fundamental Analysis
              Historical Analysis

Technically Strong Market
    A market of rising prices and large volume when general price level is also rising.

    See: *Technically Weak Market*

Technically Weak Market
    A market of declining prices and large volume when general price level is also declining.

    See: *Technically Strong Market*

Technical Rally
    A sudden upward movement of prices reacting to market news rather than supply and demand. The market catches and fills resting orders, such as stop loss orders. Once these orders are filled, the direction of the market returns to a normal position (rallying or declining as necessary).

Temporary Asset Hedge

A futures hedge in which a bank borrows long-term money and sells futures in order to lock rates in. The futures is closed out upon establishment of an appropriate deposit.

See: *Temporary Liability Hedge*

Temporary Liability Hedge

A futures hedge in which a bank makes a long-term loan and sells futures to lock rates in. The futures is closed out upon establishment of an appropriate deposit or replacement of the loan.

See: *Temporary Asset Hedge*

Tender

An offer to pay a debt or satisfy a contractual obligation.

An act in which the holder of a short futures contract gives notice of intent to deliver the physical commodity in satisfaction of the futures contract.

A tender notice is given to the respective clearing house, which in turn advises the receiving long.

See: *Retender*

Tender Price

The settlement price used to determine the invoice value on futures delivery. The procedure in the futures market is to use the settlement price of the previous night as the tender price of the delivery notice.

Example:

Settlement Prices of Spot Contract	
Date	Price
May 9	7510
May 10	7490 (used to price notice)
May 11	7560 (prepared and issued notice this day)
May 12	7570 (notice stopped)

Note: The identical settlement price is used to close out the short position of the deliverer.

The offer-to-buy price.

Example: Company ABC offers to buy outstanding shares of a Company XZY at 56.00.

Terminal

A central point at which shippers and distributors meet to exchange goods.

A term for London markets.

Terminal Elevator

A private or public grain storage facility located within a major marketing center.

Example:
Chicago, Illinois
Kansas City, Missouri or Kansas
Toledo, Ohio

Term(s)

Conditions or stipulations stated in a contract or agreement.

A period(s) of time.

Term Price

See: *Contract Price*

Tick

See: *Basis Point/Minimum Price Fluctuation/Point*

Ticker

A remote telegraphic printer that records prices, volume, and other trading and market information on a paper ribbon (ticker tape).

Ticker Symbol

An abbreviation of a commodity title (name) created by the exchange trading the respective commodity contract to simplify order and price transmissions.

Example:

Commodity	Ticker Symbol
Soybean Meal	SM
Feeder Cattle	FC
Plywood	PY
British Pounds	BP
Silver	SI
Leaded Gasoline	HR

Time and Price Discretion Order

A market or limit order to buy or sell a specified number of futures or option contracts with the floor broker given the authority to exercise his/her own judgment or discretion as to time and price of execution.

Example:

Buy 3 May N.Y. Silver broker discretion

Time and Sale

The statistics on a group of trading events; the number of times a particular price was hit and in what sequence. The exchange provides a listing as part of the permanent record.

Example:

Time	Quantity	Price
9:05	1	4331
9:06	5	4332
	2	4331
	3	4331
	10	4332
9:07	1	4331
	2	4330

See: *Time of Sale*

Time Bill/Draft

A bill of exchange or a draft payable at a specific time in the future.

See: *Demand*

Time Bracket

A time segment of the trading session, as predetermined by the authorized exchange.

Time brackets are used to maintain order and control in clearing the transactions, as well as for compliance review.

Brackets may be in any consistent length and divide the trading session into two or more time zones.

Example:

Trade Interval	Recording Code
8:30 – 9:00	A
9:00 – 9:30	B
9:30 – 10:00	C
10:00 – 10:30	D

Note: The recording code is part of the trade data submitted to the clearing house to clear the trade.

Also known as: *Trade Bracket*

See: *Bracketing*

Time (clock) Stamp

An imprint on an order in which the times the order is received and executed are affixed by a timing device (clock).

Example:

XYZ Corp
Mar 21 8X 09:01 a.m.

Note: Some stamps also identify the location and/or show the seconds as well as hour and minutes.

Time Deposit

An interest-bearing bank deposit that cannot be withdrawn until a specified day or an elapsed period of time. Advance notice is usually also required and penalties are incurred if the commitments are not met.

Example: C.D. certificate.

Time of Sale

The time and date a particular sale was executed and/or received by the exchange reporter.

See: *Time and Sale*

Time Order

A time contingency order. Instructions are given to execute the order at a given time.

Example:

Sell 1 Dec Gold Opening Only

This order is to be executed during the opening period. If execution is not fulfilled, the order is immediately cancelled.

Buy 3 Dec Gold Market On Close

This order is to be executed during the closing period.

Buy 5 Dec Gold 430.00 Good Till 10:30 a.m.

This order may be executed at 430.00 or better up to 10:30 a.m. If it is not filled, the order is automatically cancelled at 10:31 a.m.

Note: The order designates the length of time before cancelling, which is always short of extending into the next business day.

Time Value

The value of an option not including the intrinsic value. Time value is the amount a buyer is willing to pay for an out-of-the-money option (the premium) on the chance it will become profitable or the amount the buyer of an in-the-money option is willing to pay in excess in anticipation that the option will move further in-the-money. Time value declines until expiration.

Example: On June 28, August COMEX Gold call 400 is selling at .70 and August Gold futures is trading at 375.00.

Futures	375.00
Call Strike	400.00
	25.00

or $2,500.00 out-of-the-money. This option has no intrinsic value. Therefore, the price of .70 paid for the option reflects mostly time value.

Also, on June 28 an August COMEX Gold call 400 is selling at 14.30 and an August Gold futures is trading at 410.00.

Futures	410.00
Call Strike	400.00
Intrinsic value	10.00

or $1,000.00 in-the-money

Option Price	14.30	(or $1,430.00 premium)
Excess Premium	4.30	time value factor

This option has an intrinsic value of $1,000.00 (market price of the futures less option strike price). The premium price of $1,430.00 is in excess of intrinsic value. This excess reflects the remaining time value (current date June to expiration in August).

Title

The means, generally in the form of a document, that evidences formal ownership and legal rights to property.

Example:
Bill of Sale
Deed
Registration certificate

TN

The standard abbreviation for *transferable notice*, a document issued by a seller stating time, price, quantity, and brand or grade of the commodity to be delivered in fulfillment of a futures contract.

Today this term is being adopted to mean *tender notice*, which is the delivery notice. The transferable notice is the delivery notice, except that it extends a privilege that is rapidly becoming extinct—to trade out of the position and deliver it to another party during the trading session that the notice was received. This is also referred to as passing a notice. Only a few markets permit transfers or passings.

Example:
New York Cotton
New York Cocoa

Note: A transferable notice is not to be confused with a retender. A transferable notice is transferred within the same trading session as received. A retender is executed as of a following day of receiving a notice.

To Arrive Contract

A prearranged, deferred shipment in which the price is negotiated based on the cash market at the point of destination at the time of arrival. Inventory movement is guaranteed to the seller, and inventory availability is guaranteed to the buyer.

Originally, the agreement was to transfer price risk during the time of transporting grains. The seller being anxious to contract would pay the freight to destination.

Example: A flour miller requires a specified amount of wheat the first week of each month. A contract is entered that provides one (1) railcar delivered each month price based on Toledo switching district.

January	received 1 car price	3.45
February	received 1 car price	3.45
March	received 1 car price	3.44
April	received 1 car price	3.43

Today's Trade

A trade executed and entered on the current day.

Also known as: *Top Day Trade*

See: *Day Trade*
As-of Trade

Top Day Trade

See: *Today's Trade*

Track Country Station

A grain storage facility outside the terminal marketing center. It is usually in close proximity to the production area. Practice is for the freight cost from the track country station to final destination to be absorbed by the seller.

Trade

The act of buying and selling.

The buy or sell position.

An exchange of an item of value for another item of value.

Trade Account

See: *Hedge Account*

Trade Balance

The difference between value of a given country's exports and imports.

Trade Blotter

An accounting report produced by the brokerage firm listing all the trade activity that took place on a given day.

The report may be prepared randomly or grouped as to commodity, buy/sell, etc. The report may reflect "as of" and top day together or as separate reports.

Trade Bracket

See: *Time Bracket*

Trade Deficit

A larger volume of imports than exports.

See: *Trade Surplus*

Traded Option

An option that can be traded out or closed out against an opposite contract of that commodity, month, and strike price, as well as settled via exercise or abandonment.

Example:
New York COMEX Gold option
Chicago Board of Trade T-bond option
Futures Exchange Composite Index option

See: *Nontraded Option*

Trade Price

The price agreed to between buyer and seller in the trading ring and at which the trade or transaction is executed.

Example:

Futures	Trade Price
Buy 1 Nov Heating Oil	@ 8037

Option	
Buy 1 Dec S&P 500 Put 150 @ 2.05	

See: *Settlement*

Trader

An individual who buys and sells for profit or as an occupation.

See: *Broker*
  Executing Broker/Floor Broker/Pit Trader
  Floor Trader/Market Maker

Trade Surplus

A larger volume of exports than imports.

A favorable balance of trade.

Trading Account

See: *Account*

Sometimes a trading account is one in which there is daily activity or short-term transactions rather than long-term transactions.

This term is also used to differentiate a speculative account from a hedge account.

Note: A trading account is not to be confused with a trade account (hedge).

Trading Card

A document (card or multipart form) upon which each completed transaction is recorded by the executing broker. This document constitutes the original record.

Contents vary by exchange. Minimum information is as follows:

  Bought or Sold
  Number of Contracts
  Commodity and Month/Year
  Price
  Opposite Broker
  Time

Trading Differential

See: *Differential*

Trading Floor

See: *Exchange Floor*

Trading Limit

The maximum price movement permitted by a given exchange for one trading session.

Example:
COMEX Gold 2500 points above or below the previous day's settlement price.

When used in this way, this term is also known as *maximum price fluctuation.*

The maximum contracts (positions) that can be held at one time by a given holder.

Example:

Trading Limit	100 contracts

Note: The broker may stipulate positions by contract month, commodity, or entire account.

The maximum margin requirements a broker will permit a customer to hold. This limitation is similar to the maximum contract application except that it is expressed in thousands of dollars and is weighted against the full margin requirement of the account.

Example:

Trading Limit	$25,000.00

Trading Unit	The standard quantity of a given commodity stipulated by a contract.
Trading Volume	The number of contracts that changed hands during a given period of time.
Traffic	Goods moving in commerce from origin to destination.
	A division of a physical commodity operation responsible for all activity, documents, etc.
Transaction	The execution of a contract/agreement.
Transaction Fee	**See:** *Clearing Fee* *Commission Fee*
Transfer	The legal conveyance of title or property.
	Moving a futures or option position from one broker to another.
Transferable Notice	**See:** *TN*
Transfer Trade	**See:** *Ex-pit*
	The form or paperwork involved in processing an ex-pit trade.
Transmittal Letter	An export document that lists the particulars of a shipment, along with a record of documents transmitted and any special instructions, such as disposition of documents.
Trend	The general direction of a market price, higher or lower.
Trending Down	**See:** *Down Trend*
Trending Up	A price pattern established by ascending low prices. Two or more lower limits when connected by a straight line form a trend line in an upward direction. See Illustration T-1.
	Also known as: *Up Trend*
	See: *Down Trend/Trending Down*
Trend Line	On a bar chart, a straight line connecting two or more points in a price pattern emphasizing the direction of the market. See Illustration T-2.
Trial Balance	An accounting document showing a group of general ledger or customer accounts in a preselected sequence, along with current closing balance.
	Note: No accounting detail is shown.
Trier	**See:** *Sample*
Truckload	A measure used to set highway cargo rates.
Trust	A right or interest held by one or more parties for another party or parties.
Trust Receipt	A receipt with no value in itself, given in exchange for a document of value and used as a promise to pay when the contract is settled. Goods are released, but not the title, via this document.

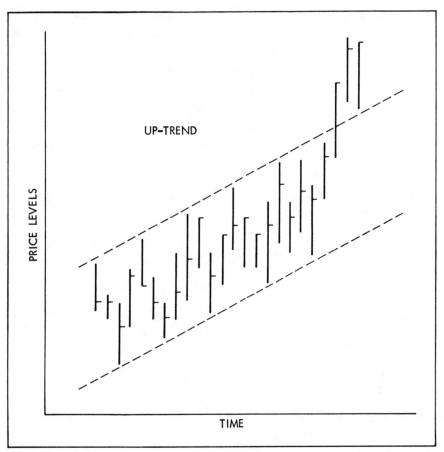

Illustration T-1

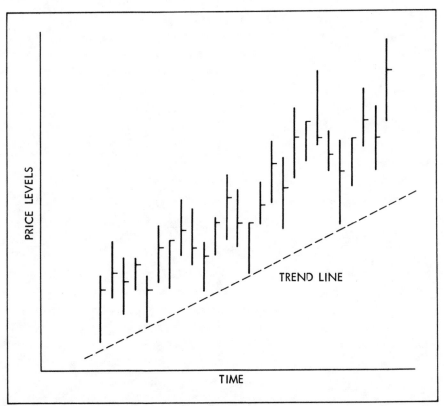

179   Illustration T-2

Two-Dollar Broker   A floor broker who handles orders for brokers for a fee based on transactions. This term originated in the securities markets and is rarely used in commodities.

Note: Floor-brokerage rates vary by exchange, commodity, and individual broker.

See: *Broker*
Carrying Broker
Executing Broker/Floor Broker/Pit Trader

Uncovered

See: *Naked*

Underlying Futures

The futures contract that may be received upon exercise of an option.

Example:

Long 1 Oct Sugar #11 Call @ 18

The buyer of this option has the right to one long October sugar futures contract at a price of 18¢ a pound at any time between the date of purchase and the date that the option expires.

Underwrite

The execution and delivery of an insurance policy.

To insure or assume the risks of insurance.

Used loosely to mean guarantee or assume responsibility for.

Underwriter

See: *Insurer*

Undisclosed (Omnibus) Account

An omnibus account in which the names of the owners are not known. This account is in the broker's name only.

See: *Disclosed (Omnibus) Account*

Unfilled Orders

A backlog of orders received but not executed; the orders received during a trading session out of range or in quantities greater than those trading at various prices.

Open orders (GTC) that are not reached by the market range.

Example: The market range is 4500–4590. Unfilled orders include

Sell 10 @ 4590 (unable—not enough contracts bought to fill all offerings)
Buy 10 @ 4490 (market never traded that low)
Buy 5 @ 4550   (market never traded at 4550 after the order was received)

Uniform Bill of Lading	A standard form used by shippers that is acceptable to all freight carriers.
United States Department of Agriculture	The federal department responsible for multiple agencies that, in turn, administer rural development, marketing and consumer services, commodity programs, conservation, research, and education, in addition to economic research, lending, and statistical reporting. This term is also known by the standard abbreviation *USDA*.
Unmatched (Trade)	**See:** *Break*
Unrealized Profits/Losses	**See:** *Paper Profits/Losses*
Unregulated	**See:** *Nonregulated Commodity*
Unsecured	A debit balance with no open or unliquidated positions. **See:** *Debit Balance* *Deficit* A debt instrument backed by good faith rather than collateral.
Unwinding	The closing out of a spread.
Upswing	An upward turn in the market or prices after a decline. See Illustration U-1.

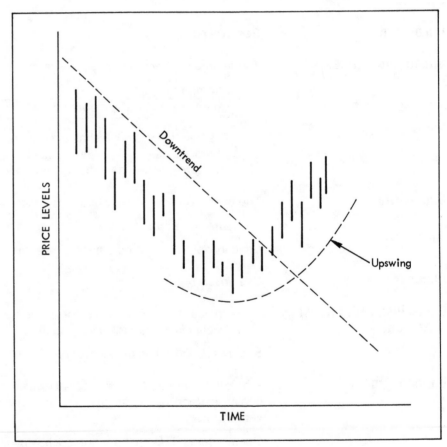

Illustration U-1

Uptick	**See:** *Plus Tick*
Up Trend	**See:** *Trending Up*
USDA	**See:** *United States Department of Agriculture*

Valuation

The process of establishing the value of an asset.

The established value of an asset.

Example:

100 oz gold worth $380 per oz = $38,000 valuation

Value

Worth or price at current market conditions.

Variable Limits

A price-limit system that allows for maximum price movements other than some preestablished standard. Variable limits give the market place more elasticity during extended chaotic market moves caused by extraordinary events.

Note: Each exchange has its own rules on when and how variable limits are activated.

Example: The normal daily limit is 200 points from previous day's settlement.

After two consecutive days of limit movement, the daily limit will be 150% of 200 for the next two sessions.

			Permitted Range
	1st day	4400	4200—4600
Limit day	2nd day	4600	4400—4800
Limit day	3rd day	4800	4600—5000
Variable	4th day	5100	4500—5100*
Variable	5th day	5350**	4800—5400*

* Days the variable limit rule was used.
**Day the market failed to close limit up. The market reverts back to normal limits.

The basic purpose is to broaden the trading range to fulfill the influx of orders. Market pressure is relieved.

Note: Individual exchange policies must be checked in an exchange's rule book.

Variation Allowance	**See:** *Maintenance Level*
Variation Margin	**See:** *Maintenance Margin*
Variation Margin Call	**See:** *Maintenance Margin Call*
Venture Capital	High-risk-investment capital, generally used in establishment of a new business or product. Venture capital generally comes from private sources rather than from banks or investment establishments.
Vertical Bear Call Spread	**See:** *Bear Call (Spread)*
Vertical Bear Put Spread	**See:** *Bear Put (Spread)*
Vertical Bull Call Spread	**See:** *Bull Call (Spread)*
Vertical Bull Put Spread	**See:** *Bull Put (Spread)*
Vertical Spread	A long option position paired for margin purposes with a short option with the same expiration but different exercise prices.

Example:

Buy 1 Dec T-bond Call @ 68
Sell 1 Dec T-bond Call @ 66

See: *Horizontal Spread*

Visible Item	Tangible goods traded.

Example: Soybeans, delivered as beans, are visible; whereas S & P Index, delivered in cash, is not, for an index is an intangible item.

Visible Supply	Goods physically accountable in a warehouse.

Loosely, goods accountable on a farm, in an elevator, or in transit.

That which can be counted.

Vital Commodity	A commodity that generally cannot be substituted and is essential to support life and maintain a system of commerce.

Example:
Grains
Fibers
Metals (aluminum through zinc)
Fuels

See: *Basic Commodities*
Stockpile Commodities

Volatility	A measurement of the degree to which price fluctuations take place.
Volume (of trade)	**See:** *Trading Volume*
Voucher	A document evidencing receipt or payment.
Vs. Cash	**See:** *AA/Against Actuals*
Vs. Trade	**See:** *Special Vs. (Trade)*

Wait and Instruct   See: *Instruct*

Warehouse   See: *Depository*

Warehouse Receipt   See: *Depository Receipt*

Warehouse Receipt Loan   A loan the collateral for which is a warehouse receipt.

Wash Invoice   An invoice that cancels a previous invoice while providing documentation of the transaction. A wash invoice offsets two contracts, neither of which should have been performed (making and taking delivery).

Also known as: *Washout Invoice*

Washout Invoice   See: *Wash Invoice*

Wash Sale   A purchase and sale done by the same person or persons at the same price to create volume and price activity. This transaction is "fictitious" and is forbidden by government and exchange regulations.

Wasting Asset   An asset that disappears or loses value with the passing of time.

> **Example:** Consider a long option, put or call. The time-value portion of the option premium diminishes with the passage of time. At the point of expiration, all at- or out-of-the-money options will have no time-value premium.
>
> Consider, too, crude oil. Once welled and refined, crude oil cannot be replaced. Supplies (natural reserves) diminish each year.

Waybill

A detailed, written description of a shipment issued by a carrier.

In the stictest sense, goods transported via rail.

See: *Inland Bill of Lading/Pro*

Weak Basis

A condition in which the spot price is significantly below the futures, indicating a low demand or an oversupply.

Also known as: *Wide Basis*

> **Example:** On a given day, corn is trading at $3.08 per bushel in the *cash* market. (The normal basis is .08¢.)
>
> Futures and cash prices will tend to move up or down together but may do so in unequal amounts because of technical conditions.
>
> If on that given day, corn is trading at $3.24 per bushel in the *futures* market, the wide basis is considered weak, for it is expected that a 16¢ basis will not persist.

See: *Narrow Basis/Strong Basis*

Weak Hands

A poorly capitalized trader who may not be expected to withstand adverse price movements.

Weather Market

An erratic market influenced by actual or predicted weather occurrences.

Wet Delivery

A procedure that allows the long to post cash or T-bills in the amount of the contract and receive immediate delivery upon payment to seller rather than receiving a receipt for subsequent presentation before receiving delivery.

"W" Formation

See: *Double Bottom*

Whip Saw

The reversing of a position, generally on technical happenings, thereby creating losses on both transactions. This action is most commonly experienced by traders trading the market too closely or trading in a narrow market.

> **Example:**
>
> | Buy at | 360 | |
> |---|---|---|
> | Sell stop | 350 and go short | 350 |
> | Buy at | | 360 |
> | | 10-point loss | 10-point loss |

The trader went long at 360, believing that if stopped at 350 a short position is warranted. The market, on a technical note, activated the 350 stops. Once the selling subsided, the market rose to 360 again. The trader has been whip-sawed.

Wide Basis

See: *Weak Basis*

Winter Spread

A seasonal spread in the energy market in which heating oil is the product spread with crude oil.

> **Example:**
>
> Buy 1 Dec Heating Oil
> Sell 1 Dec Crude Oil

See: *Crack Spread*
Summer Crack Spread

Wirehouse

A commission house operating a private wire or communications network to branch offices or correspondent firms.

> **Example:**
> E.F. Hutton
> Dean Witter Reynolds
> Prudential Bache

Wireroom

The central location of a brokerage house, where communication lines merge; orders are disseminated to the appropriate exchanges and executions are reported back to the original senders.

World Market

A market influenced by global supply and demand, subject to such trading barriers as are erected by governments from time to time.

Writer

See: *Grantor*

x-Axis

The horizontal standard on a graph or chart that uses a system of coordinates. See Illustration X-1.

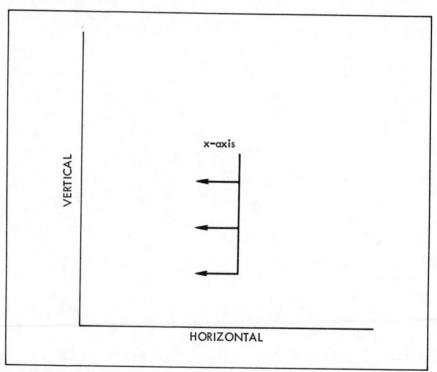

Illustration X-1

See: *y-axis*

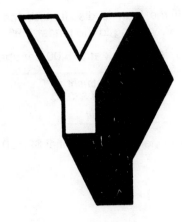

y-Axis

The vertical standard on a graph or chart that uses a system of coordinates. See Illustration Y-1.

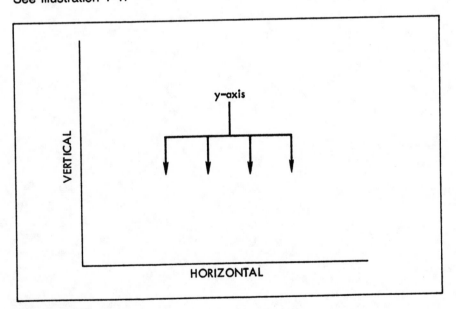

Illustration Y-1

See: *x-axis*

Yield

The return or profit on an investment.

Example: Lend $10,000.00 at 9% for 1 year. The interest earned is $900.00, or a 9% yield.

Note: If the loan is discounted, the lender will give the borrower only $9,100.00, yielding to the lender 9.9%.

Buy ABC stock at $25.00 per share

Investment (100 shares)	$2,500.00
Sell at $30.00	3,000.00
Profit	500.00 = 20% yield

Note: The yield is on the initial $2,500 investment.

Zero Minus Tick

A sale in which the price moves down from that of one or more sales at the same price.

See: *Minus Tick*
Zero Plus Tick

Zero Plus Tick

A sale in which the price moves up from that of one or more sales at the same price.

See: *Plus Tick*
Zero Minus Tick

Futures

Reading the tables:

Determine the general category of the commodity.

Example:
Grains & Oilseeds
Metals & Petroleum
Financial
Stock Indexes

Find the specific commodity.

Example:

FUTURES PRICES

	Open	High	Low	Settle	Change	Lifetime High	Lifetime Low	Open Interest
			METALS & PETROLEUM					
Jan	302.70	302.70	301.60	301.40	1.20	333.50	301.60	33
Est. vol 33,000		vol Wed 34,200			open int 170,285			+2,876

Line 1	**Commodity**	Gold
	Exchange	CMX (Commodity Exchange, New York)
	Contract Size	100 troy oz.
	Price Quoted	$ per troy oz.

Find the line with the delivery month in question.

Read the information by column as follows:

Column 1	**Delivery Month**	The month the contract is due. • Contracts are referred to as: *January gold* • Contract delivery dates extend into the next year: *Fb (February) 86*
Column 2	**Open**	The price at the opening of the market for the day.
Column 3	**High**	The highest trade price of the day.
Column 4	**Low**	The lowest trade price of the day.
Column 5	**Settle**	The final price(s) of day.
Column 6	**Change**	The amount up/down from the previous trading day's settle price.
Column 7	**Lifetime High**	The highest price traded in the life of that contract month. • This column is sometimes labeled *Season High*.
Column 8	**Lifetime Low**	The lowest price traded in the life of that contract month. • This column is sometimes labeled *Season Low*.
Column 9	**Open Interest**	Number of contracts outstanding, or not offset by delivery or offsetting trade.

The line at the bottom of the tabulation gives the estimated volume of all gold contracts traded on the New York Commodity Exchange on this day, the previous day's actual volume, the total open interest, and the net change in open interest from the previous day (not including today's volume).

Using the information:

To determine the value of the contract, multiply the price quoted by 100 (100 troy oz.).

Example: One contract of August 1986 Gold is ($351.00 × 100) $35,100.00.

Full value is rarely exchanged. The amount is due only if actual delivery/acceptance is made. An initial margin or good faith deposit to carry the contract is required: as the market fluctuates, additional or maintenance margin may be required.

Individual brokerage fees also apply.

192

OPTIONS

Heavily traded options are listed under **Futures Options**. Less frequently, traded options may be found under **Other Futures Options** or individual exchange advertisements.

Foreign currency options are given in an additional table as well.

Reading the tables:

Find the specific commodity.

Example:

FUTURES OPTIONS

GOLD (CMX)—100 troy ounces: dollars per troy ounce

Strike Price	Calls—Last			Puts—Last		
	Feb	Apr	Jun	Feb	Apr	Jun
280	....	....	....	60	....	....

Est vol. 11,000. Wed vol. 2,425 calls, 4,085 puts
Open interest Wed. 61,405 calls, 32,110 puts

Line 1	**Commodity**	Gold
	Exchange	CMX (Commodity Exchange, New York)
	Contract Size	100 troy oz.
	Price Quoted	Dollars per troy oz. (for the right to acquire a futures contract)

Read the information by column as follows:

Column 1	**Strike Price**	The guaranteed futures price, should the option be exercised. • Incremental price levels are given above and below current futures price.
Column 2–4	**Calls—Last (Traded Months)**	The final price traded for the day in each futures contract month, at each strike level for a call. • Strike prices not traded are indicated by dots (....), as in *Feb call at a 280 strike*. • This column is sometimes labeled *Settle*.
Column 5–7	**Puts—Last (Traded Months)**	The final price traded for the day in each futures contract month, at each strike level for a put. • Strike prices not trades are indicated by dots (....), as in *Apr. put at a 280 strike*. • This column is sometimes labeled *Settle*.

The first line at the bottom of the tabulation gives the estimated volume of all gold option contracts (puts plus calls) sold on the New York Commodity Exchange on this day and the previous day's actual volume by calls and puts.

The second line at the bottom gives the previous day's open interest by call and put.

Using the information:
To determine the premium that an option buyer pays to the writer (seller) of the option, multiply the price at the given strike price level by 100 (100 troy oz.).

Example:
Premium for one April Call at the 320 strike level is ($4.00 × 100) $400.00.

Premium for one April Put at the 320 strike level is ($16.70 × 100) $1670.00.

The buyer's risk is limited to this amount. Individual brokerage fees also apply.

The seller is responsible for any margin requirements plus individual brokerage fees.

CASH PRICES

Reading the tables:

Determine the general category of the commodity.

Examples:
Grains & Feeds
Metals
Precious Metals

Find the specific commodity.

Examples:

CASH PRICES
PRECIOUS METALS

Gold, troy oz.
Krugerrand, whol a312.50   313.25   388.50

Line 1	**Commodity unit for price**	Gold troy oz.

Find the specified type.

Column 1	**Current Day**	Quote as of 4 p.m. EST of previous day.
Column 2	**Previous day**	Quote as of 4 p.m. EST 2 trading days ago.
Column 3	**Years ago**	Quote as of last year.

Using the information:
To determine price for each unit.

Example: Read the quote as: One gold Krugerrand asking price is $312.50.

Basic Calculations

BASIS OF A COMMODITY

Basis = Difference between spot and futures

Example:

Spot	$5.20
Futures	$5.50
Basis = $5.50 − $5.20	
Basis = $ .30 futures premium	

BASIS OF A CURRENCY (FX MARKET)

$$\text{Basis} = \frac{\text{Spot} \times (\text{Eurodollar} - \text{Eurocurrency})}{100} \times \frac{\text{Number of Days to Maturity}}{360 \text{ or } 365}$$

Example: For British pounds:

Trade date	March 15
Delivery date	June 15
Eurocurrency rates	
Dollar	19⅜% bid
Pound	17⅞% offer
Spot British pound	2.1725

$$\text{Basis} = \frac{2.1725 \times (19.375 - 17.875)}{100} \times \frac{91}{365}$$

$$= \frac{296.54625}{36500}$$

$$= .0081 \text{ premium or } \$202.50/$$
Contract 25,000

EQUITY/DEFICIT

Equity/Deficit = Cash + Open Positions Marked to Market (difference between profits/ losses)

Example

		Case 1	Case 2
Ledger balance		$500.00 Cr	$700.00 Cr
Open positions			
Long 1 Oct COMEX Gold	@ 394.00		
Settlement	396.00	200.00 Cr	200.00 Cr
Short 1 Dec COMEX Gold	@ 394.00		
Short 1 Dec COMEX Gold	@ 396.00		
Settlement	408.00	800.00 Dr	800.00 Dr
		$100.00 Dr	$100.00 Cr
		Deficit	Equity

A credit value after requirements is subtracted from equity is the excess.

IN-THE-MONEY/LOAN VALUE

In-the-Money/Loan Value = (Difference between Strike Price and the Futures Settlement) × Factor × Quantity

Example:

Long 1 April Gold Call @ Strike price		$ 400.00
	Futures Settlement	$ 450.00
In-the-Money/Loan Value = ($450.00 − $400.00) × 100 × 1		
In-the-Money/Loan Value = $5,000.00		

Application of Loan Value

Long 1 April Gold Call @ Strike price		$ 400.00
Short 1 April Gold	Trade price	$ 420.00
	Futures Settlement	$ 450.00
Market value of futures		$45,000.00
Short value of sale (futures)		42,000.00
	Variation margin due	3,000.00
Loan value (available)		$ 5,000.00
	Variation margin due (excess)	-0-

OUT-OF-THE-MONEY

Out-of-the-Money = (Difference between Futures Settlement and Option Strike) × Factor × Quantity

Example:

Feb COMEX GOLD put	
Futures settlement	$400.00
Strike prices	$380.00
Out-of-the-money put = ($400.00 − $380.00) × 100 × 1	
Out-of-the-money put = $2,000.00	

Note: A call is out-of-the-money at $420.00 strike.

INTRINSIC VALUE

Intrinsic Value (call) = Difference Futures is above Strike
Intrinsic Value (put) = Difference Futures is below Strike

Example:

Feb COMEX GOLD	
Option Strike	Futures Price
$380.00	
$400.00	$400.00
$420.00	

A long call at $380 is profitable to exercise; a long put at $420 is profitable to exercise.

Futures	$400.00	LG Put	$420.00
LG Call	380.00	Futures	400.00
	$ 20.00 per oz.		$ 20.00 per oz.

MARKET VALUE

Market Value = Settlement Price × Factor × Quantity

Example: Long 3 NYFE Composite

Settlement Price	$68.00	OR	6800 Points
	$ 500		5.00 Factor
Market Value = 6800 × 5.00 × 3			
Market Value = $102,000.00			

MARK-TO-MARKET

Futures/Profit or Loss
Profit/Loss = Difference between Trade Price and Settlement Price × Factor × Quantity

Example:

Short 2 Dec COMEX Gold @ $396.40
Long 2 Dec COMEX Gold @ $396.40

Settlement price $396.00
Profit/loss = ($396.40 − $396.00) × 100 × 2
Profit/loss = $ 80.00

Short 2 Dec COMEX Gold = $80.00 Profit
Long 2 Dec COMEX Gold = $80.00 Loss

The realized profit/loss at closeout includes commissions/fees.

Options/Premium Market Value
Premium Market Value = Option Settlement × Factor × Quantity

Example: Sugar #11

Settlement price call @ 11.00	3.05	(305 pts)
Factor	1120	11.20
Contracts	1	1

Premium Market Value = 305 × $11.20 × 1
= $3,416.00

PREMIUM

Premium = Trade Price of Option × Factor × Quantity

Example: Bought 1 Oct Sugar 11 Call @ 18   Trade price 1.75
Premium = 1.75 × 1120 × 1
= $1,960.00

TIME VALUE

Example: August COMEX Gold Call @ 400   Trade price .70

August COMEX Gold Futures 375.00	
Futures	$ 375.00
Call strike	400.00
	$ 25.00 Out-of-the-money

This option has no intrinsic value. The price of .70 reflects mostly time value.

Example: December COMEX Gold Call @ 400 Trade price 14.30

December Comex Gold Futures 410.00	
Futures	$ 400.00
Call Strike	410.00
	$ 10.00 In-the-money
Intrinsic value	$1,000.00
Option premium	1,430.00
Excess premium	
Time value	$ 430.00

How to
Find a Commodity Factor

To find the factor of a given commodity, determine how trading in the commodity is expressed in the financial pages of the newspaper and apply one of the following simple formulas:

Price quoted in dollars per trading unit:

$$\text{Quantity} \div 100 = \text{Factor}$$

Example:

Soybean Meal — 100 tons; $ a ton
100 (tons) ÷ 100 = 1.00

Commodity trades in a fraction (1/4, 1/8, 1/16, 1/32, 1/64):

$$\frac{\text{Quantity} \div 100}{\text{Denominator of Fraction}} = \text{Factor}$$

Example:

CORN 5,000 bu; $ per bu (prices in 1/4s)
$$\frac{(5,000 \div 100)}{4} = 12.50$$

Price quoted in dollars for a given number of units per trading unit:

$$\text{Quantity} \div \text{Number of Units} = \text{Factor}$$

Example:

Lumber — 100,000 bd ft; $ per 1000 bd ft.
100,000 ÷ 1,000 = 100.00

Price quoted in cents per trading unit:

$$\frac{\text{Quantity} \div 100 \text{ (dollars)}}{100 \text{ (cents)}} = \text{Factor}$$

Example:

Soybean Oil — 60,000 lb.; per lbs.
$$\frac{(60,000 \div 100)}{100} = \$6.00$$

Price quoted in foreign currency per trading unit:

$$\text{Quantity} \div 100,000 = \text{Factor}$$

Example:

Swiss Franc — 125,000 francs; $ per franc
125,000 ÷ 100,000 = 1.25

Price quoted for financial futures:

$$\frac{(\text{Quantity} \div 100)}{4 \text{ (90-day units)}} = \text{Factor}$$

Example:

T Bills — $ million; pts of 100%
$$\frac{(1,000,000 \div 100)}{4} = 25.00$$

Note: The market price is based on a 90-day discount rate. As the contract size represents four 90-day units, that number is used in the formula.

TICKER SYMBOLS

Current Calendar Months:

F January	K May	U September
G February	M June	V October
H March	N July	X November
J April	Q August	Z December

Second-Year or "Red Months"

A January	E May	P September
B February	I June	R October
C March	L July	S November
D April	O August	T December

Third-year symbols consist of current calendar month plus a year indicator.

EXCHANGES

ACE	AMEX Commodity Exchange
AMEX	American Stock Exchange
AMM	Associative Mercantile Market (a division of the CME)
CBT/CBOT	Chicago Board of Trade
CBOE	Chicago Board Options Exchange
CME/the Merc	Chicago Mercantile Exchange
ComEx/COMEX/CMX	(New York) Commodity Exchange, Inc.
CRCE	Chicago Rice and Cotton Exchange
CSC/CSCE	New York Coffee, Sugar and Cocoa Exchange, Inc.
CTN/NYCE	New York Cotton Exchange
EOE	European Options Exchange
HKCE	Hong Kong Commodity Exchange
IMM	International Monetary Market (a division of the CME)
INTEX	International Futures Exchange (Bermuda) Ltd.
IPE	International Petroleum Exchange of London Ltd.
KCBT/KC	Kansas City Board of Trade
KLCE	Kuala Lumpur Commodity Exchange (Malaysia)
LCE	London Commodity Exchange
LGFM	London Gold Futures Market
LIFFE/LIFE	London International Financial Futures Exchange
LME	London Metal Exchange
MACE/MCE/MidAm	MidAmerica Commodity Exchange
ME	Montreal Exchange
MGE/MLPS	Minneapolis Grain Exchange
NYCE	New York Cotton Exchange
NYFE	New York Futures Exchange
NYMEX/The New York Merc/NYME	New York Mercantile Exchange
NYSE/the Big Board	New York Stock Exchange, Inc.
PHLX	Philadelphia Stock Exchange
SFE	Sidney Futures Exchange

SIMEX	Singapore International Monetary Exchange, Ltd.
TFE	Toronto Futures Exchange
TOCOM	Tokyo Commodity Exchange
VSE	Vancouver Stock Exchange
WCE/WPG	Winnipeg Commodity Exchange
WEE	World Energy Exchange

TRADING MARKETS

AAM	Agricultural and Associate Market
GIM	Government Instrument Market
IDEM	Index, Debt and Energy Market
COM	Commodity Option Market

RELATED ORGANIZATIONS

ACC	American Copper Association
CFTC	Commodity Futures Trading Commission
ECE	Economic Commission for Europe
FIA	Futures Industry Association
ICO	International Coffee Organization
IOCC	International Options Clearing Corp.
NAFTA	National Association of Futures Trading Advisors
NFA	National Futures Association
OCC	Options Clearing Corporation
OPEC	Organization of Petroleum Exporting Countries
SEC	Securities Exchange Commission
S & P	Standard and Poors